coolcamping
scotland

Robin McKelvie & Jenny McKelvie

with additional contributions by Andy Stothert and Keith Didcock

So what's this Cool Camping all about, then?

To us, *Cool Camping* is all about camping in very special places and this book, along with the other titles in the *Cool Camping* series, is a guide to help you find those places.

For most people, the attraction of camping is to leave their town or city behind, to get outdoors, enjoy the countryside and breathe lungfuls of good, wholesome fresh air. Dispensing with all those modern luxuries we're used to, if only for a weekend, is a refreshing and invigorating experience unmatched by even a luxury spa break.

But finding those idyllic countryside escapes is not easy, when so many campsites are being developed into commercial holiday parks. So that's where *Cool Camping* comes in. We've travelled the length and breadth of Scotland to bring you our personal choice of favourite places to pitch.

Unless otherwise stated, they're all designated campsites with the usual amenities including toilets and hot showers, but importantly, we don't judge campsites on the quality of these facilities. We leave that to other books. We're more interested in the location, the view, the surrounding area – even the philosophy and attitude of the staff and owners. We're looking at the almost immeasurable combination of factors that transforms a place from a mere campsite to a very special place to camp.

We might be swayed by a remote location, a stunning view or the fact that it's next to a tranquil loch. There might be the opportunity to camp in a tipi, wooden wigwam or roundhouse. We might recommend a delightful campsite in a hidden valley, even though the shower block has seen better days. But we'd never highlight a pristine site with fantastic facilities if that's all there is to recommend it.

One thing you can be sure of: we left all the featured campsites knowing that someday, we'd like to return. And what more of a recommendation could you want?

Cool Camping: Scotland
First published in the United Kingdom in 2007 by
Punk Publishing Ltd
3 The Yard
Pegasus Place
London
SE11 5SD

www.punkpublishing.com

www.coolcamping.co.uk

A catalogue record of this book is available from the British Library.
ISBN-10: 0-9552036-3-5
ISBN-13: 978-0-9552036-3-3

10 9 8 7 6 5 4 3 2

introduction

If your ideal camping experience is being packed shoulder to shoulder with hundreds of other poor souls, with any semblance of a view blighted by monstrous motor homes, then you probably won't want to read any further. If, on the other hand, you enjoy a more *Cool Camping* experience in characterful campsites where they treat you like a real person and you get plenty of your own space, then read on. What could be cooler than camping in one of the world's most stunningly scenic countries, whose vaulting mountains, tumbling glens and myriad islands are even more impressive in the flesh than any Hollywood blockbuster or shortbread tin could ever convey?

For first timers, or even those who think they already know Scotland, the bare statistics of this unique country might come as a bit of a surprise. Whilst England, Wales and Northern Ireland have no mountain peaks over 900 metres (the Munro mountains), Scotland boasts a whopping 284 and the country's coastline is three times larger than that of England and also more extensive than either the French or the Spanish littorals. Everyone knows there are a few islands, but did you know there were over 800? However you look at it, there is a lot out there to be explored in one of Europe's least densely populated countries, making it a perfect destination for *Cool Camping*.

We think the nominal downsides of camping in Scotland, mainly the midges and the weather, are a smokescreen cooked up by the locals to put you off coming – they want to keep it all for themselves. No one has ever caught malaria from a midge and when the weather turns it all just adds to the drama. We spent enough sun-drenched days and lingering summer evenings watching the sun set over the Atlantic to believe in the smokescreen theory. In writing this book we were impressed by the campsites on offer and the positive and unpretentious attitudes of the campsite owners. There was an encouraging lack of commercialism and a feeling that campers were being treated properly, rather than just as the source of a few extra pounds that could be squeezed between caravans.

In this book we don't hold much truck by fancy facilities and glitzy claims either.

All sites included have flush toilets and all bar one has a shower (Achnahaird p199, where you can, rather quaintly, enjoy a hot shower in the local village hall), but more importantly each one has something special about it. That may be the jaw-dropping views (there tend to be a lot of those in Scotland), a sense of escaping to somewhere truly remote, an unusual camping venue like an Iron Age roundhouse or a canvas tipi, or perhaps it's in an area bathed in history. Frequently, the recommendations have all of these, and then some.

In recent years Scotland has emerged as something of an adventure playground and camping is the perfect way to get access to all these 'new' adventure sports. In 2006, Scotland was voted by a leading mountain bike magazine as the world's best location for the sport, a timely prelude to Scotland hosting the world championships in 2007. Also on offer are world-class surfing, canyoning, whitewater rafting, windsurfing, scuba diving, kayaking and coasteering; the list goes on. Add in the well-known charms of walking and climbing – Scotland boasts everything from simple strolls and one-hour hill climbs to severe ice climbing in the Cairngorms and one of the world's great long-distance walks in the West Highland Way – and it is a compelling mix.

No book on *Cool Camping* in Scotland would be complete without also mentioning 'wild camping'. The Scots have been doing it for centuries – the Highland clans in a sense were all dedicated wild campers – but only recently have the wild camping rights been enshrined in law. At the end of this book (see p215) we have researched the vagaries of wild camping and provided a few recommended locations to get you started on your adventure, which could just be a small part of your camping trip or what you choose to do the entire time.

Whether you are camping at a site or camping in the wilds, you will seldom be disappointed in a country where it appears to be a legal requirement to have swathes of epic scenery waiting around every corner. Armed with this guide you can seek out the best venues for *Cool Camping*, away from the crowds, at sites that have each been carefully chosen for that certain something that makes camping such a deeply rewarding and enlivening way to spend your precious holiday. Enjoy.

campsite locator

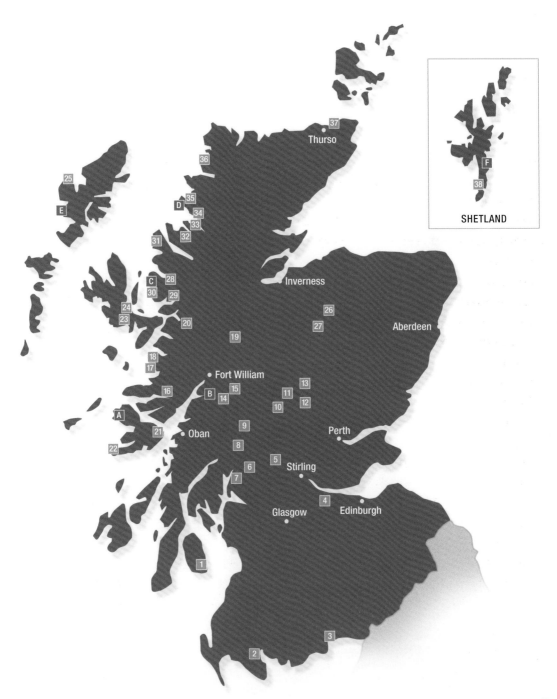

Thurso

Inverness

Aberdeen

Fort William

Perth

Oban

Stirling

Glasgow

Edinburgh

SHETLAND

1 2

3 4

cool camping top 5

The mere fact that a site features in this book is all the recommendation you need. But the best of the best? Well, there are a few that deserve the special 'Cool Camping Top 5' award. Here are our pick of the pitches.

1 achnahaird   p199

Arrive at the end of the world and stroll along the bracing Atlantic sands with two of Scotland's most dramatic mountains for company.

2 camusdarach   p95

Golden beaches, azure waters, pristine islands offshore – no it's not the Caribbean but a stunning eco-friendly campsite in northwest Scotland.

3 glenbrittle   p131

Spectacularly remote, utterly peaceful and with a dramatic mountainous vista that blocks out all mobile phone signals. Perfect.

4 applecross   p171

Sweeping views of the Isle of Skye – and one of Scotland's best pubs just a short amble away.

5= lazy duck   p149

More ducks than people in a Highland retreat where chilling is de rigueur: idle in a hammock, enjoy a 'bush shower' or steam off your stresses in the sauna.

5= cnip village grazing trust   p143

A beautiful, unspoilt coastal site owned and operated by the village residents and a very, very, very long way away from anywhere.

campsites at a glance

ON YER BIKE

Most of the sites listed have decent cycling in the near vicinity.

seal shore

Arran is geologically schizophrenic. It sits astride Scotland's Highland Boundary Fault, the geological feature that separates the rolling farmland of the Lowlands from the rugged peaks of the Highlands. So, when you disembark from the ferry at Brodick, which is appropriately in the middle of the island, you are faced with a choice. Head north and you're off into the wilds of heather-clad mountains, roaming deer and deep-cut glens. Head south and you're into undulating countryside, standing stones and sea views. Luckily, Arran is not very big and is easily explored whichever way you choose. But if you have come to Arran more for heritage than for hiking, then south is the way to go.

Seal Shore, at Kildonan on the southern tip of Arran, has one of the island's very few sandy beaches. As the name suggests, it is best known for the abundance of sea life to be spotted bobbing amongst the waves and the birdlife gliding above them. The campsite is a neat and compact little place, run by a no-nonsense couple originally from Yorkshire. It slopes gently down to the beach, which has a handy finger of black rock, known as a dolerite dyke, protruding from the sands into the water. It's ideal for

basking in the sun, as long as the seals (which may or may not be German) haven't already bagged the best spots.

The dolerite dyke is just one example of Arran's geological oddities. There are rocks on Arran formed in virtually all the geological periods of the earth, from the Cambrian to the Triassic, making Arran a geologist's treasure trove.

Bounding forward a few million years in time, Arran still has plenty to offer those who haven't packed a rock hammer in their rucksack. Kildonan is the ideal base from which to explore the island's history and its rich heritage is apparent in the very names of its attractions. Kildonan itself is named after St Donan, a 6th-century Irish monk who settled here. Out in the Sound stands the lighthouse on Pladda, a Norse name meaning 'flat isle', whilst further in the distance is the gigantic hump of Ailsa Craig, whose name comes from the Gaelic for 'fairy rock'. Above the seashore stands the ruins of a 13th-century keep, first built by the MacDonald clan, known as the Lords of the Isles. More recently, Arran was known as Clydeside's playground because it attracted hordes of holidaying dockers on their annual holidays. Back then, sailing down the Clyde to Arran for the Trades' Fortnight was known as going 'doon the water'. Those days are all long gone, as are most of the shipyards on the Clyde, but that ages-old mix of Norse and Gaelic culture with Highland and Lowland Scottish history has left its mark on southern Arran.

If you have the time then it's worth circumnavigating the island because the less-frequented western side has a number of attractions, not least the stone circle at Machrie and the faded grandeur of the Victorian Blackwaterfoot Lodge Hotel. And on the stretch of road from Lochranza in the north to Brodick you'll find another of Scotland's little slices of Cornwall: Corrie is a huddle of cottages along the road by a small harbour and is an ideal base for tackling Arran's most popular climb to the summit of Goat Fell. Its popularity lies not only in its relatively accessible summit, but also in its great vantage point to muse over the delights of this intriguing, schizophrenic little island.

THE UPSIDE: Seabirds, seals and sandcastles.

THE DOWNSIDE: The occasional howling souwesterly testing the resilience of your geodesic dome tent.

THE DAMAGE: £6 per person plus £1 for a campervan or tent. Children under 5 are free and 6–12s are £2.

THE FACILITIES: Very decent toilet block with hot showers. Dishwashing area, laundry and access to a fridge freezer. There's also a new undercover (and windproof!) cooking area and campers' day room.

NEAREST DECENT PUB: The recently refurbished Kildonan Hotel (01770 820207) is right next door and serves excellent food and decent beer. For a better range of ales but mediocre food in less salubrious surroundings, head to the Breadalbane Hotel (01770 820284) a mile to the west.

IF IT RAINS: There is a small museum at Brodick and a range of craft shops in Lamlash. The Auchrannie Hotel complex (01770 302234) also has extensive leisure facilities including an impressive swimming pool. Otherwise it's backgammon in the pub.

GETTING THERE: From Brodick follow the B841 south for 12 miles. Kildonan is signposted to the left.

PUBLIC TRANSPORT: There is a regular bus service, which stops 50 yards from the site.

OPEN: Mar–Oct.

IF IT'S FULL: There is a youth hostel (0870 004 1158) a few miles back up the road at Whiting Bay or an extremely basic campsite with no hot water or showers at Glenrosa (01770 302380) just north of Brodick.

Seal Shore Camping & Touring Site, Kildonan, Isle of Arran KA27 8SE

| | t | 01770 820320 | w | www.isleofarran.freeserve.co.uk/camp.htm |

bladnoch distillery

There are places that you never knew existed. And when you find them, the dilemma is whether to let other people in on the secret or to keep them to yourself. Dumfries and Galloway is a neglected corner of Scotland and the area around Wigtown, known as the Machars after the sandy grasslands that stretch from its rolling farmland down to the sea, is just one of Scotland's hidden treasures. Whilst it may lack some of the naked grandeur of the highlands, its pristine charm and quiet, unhurried poise is a secret bursting to get out.

The Bladnoch Distillery is a small independent maker of a rather fine single malt. Like Bladnoch itself, this place is a well-kept secret and not part of a multinational drinks conglomerate. The enthusiastic owner, Raymond Armstrong, is something of a *bon viveur* who has turned the place into a thriving little attraction in its own right. In addition to providing distillery tours, he has converted one of the old malting sheds into a small music venue, which has hosted an eclectic range of guests from deep south American bluesmen to some of Scotland's up and coming bands. Raymond once even persuaded a holidaying

American cellist to get up on stage and play in return for a few bottles of Scotch.

Camping is something of a sideline for the distillery and if you're lucky enough to be able to camp behind Raymond's house, where the sleepy River Bladnoch sidles past the distillery garden and under the old stone bridge, don't tell too many people about it. This is the sort of quietly mesmerising place where you can be forgiven for losing track of the time. Sadly, only smaller tents are allowed on the lawn. Larger tents are banished to a field behind the distillery (and even small tents are sent to the field when the garden is being used for a wedding).

The main attraction nearby is Wigtown, known as Scotland's Book Town. The town's book festivals, held twice annually in spring and autumn, have gained a growing reputation and attract an eclectic bunch of contributors from writers like Louis de Bernieres to film makers like Robin Hardy, who brought Edward Woodward and Britt Ekland here to make the cult film *The Wicker Man* in 1973. The location's sinister credentials are borne out by a memorial just outside Wigtown to two local women who were tied to a stake in the river in 1685 and drowned by the rising tide. Their crime was to support the Covenanters, the religious dissenters who refused to acknowledge the king as head of the Church.

Much of *The Wicker Man* was actually filmed south of Bladnoch at Whithorn, another fascinating little town worth stopping at on the way to the Isle of Whithorn. This striking fishing village is on the southern tip of the Machars, looking across the Solway to the Isle of Man and the west Cumbrian coast, and it has the best pub in the region, The Steam Packet Inn, where the seafood is so fresh on the plate you would swear it's still twitching.

Back at Bladnoch, there is a comfortable and attractive inn just across the road from the distillery from which to savour a pint of Belhaven ale and bask in the evening sun. And when it's time to turn in, you might just be lured back to the distillery by the sound of music from the malting shed. But be warned. Raymond has a way of sniffing out hidden musical talent, so keep quiet about your party piece or you might find yourself up on stage playing the spoons on your knees. Mind you, there might be a bottle of Scotch in it for you.

THE UPSIDE: Peaceful garden site by the silent waters of the Bladnoch river.

THE DOWNSIDE: Larger tents are confined to the main campsite in an undistinguished field behind the distillery.

THE DAMAGE: £6 per night for two adults; £1 per extra person. Under-5s go free. Prices include electrical hook-ups for caravans.

THE FACILITIES: Only two showers and one toilet cubicle each for ladies and gents housed above the distillery shop. Additional toilets available downstairs during shop hours.

NEAREST DECENT PUB: The Bladnoch Inn (01988 402200), just across the road from the distillery serves a decent pint of Belhaven ale and above-average food, but The Steam Packet Inn (01988 500334) at the Isle of Whithorn is well worth the trip.

IF IT RAINS: Head into Wigtown to browse in the many second-hand bookshops and stop for tea in Readinglasses, opposite the village green.

GETTING THERE: From the M74 follow the A75 to Newton Stewart and turn left on the A714. After 6 miles, turn right for Bladnoch and the distillery is on the right just before the bridge.

OPEN: Easter–Oct.

IF IT'S FULL: Knock School Caravan Park (01988 700414) at Monreith, about 14 miles south of Bladnoch has a tiny, secluded area for tents.

Bladnoch Distillery, Bladnoch, Wigtown DG8 9AB	t 01988 402605	w www.bladnoch.co.uk

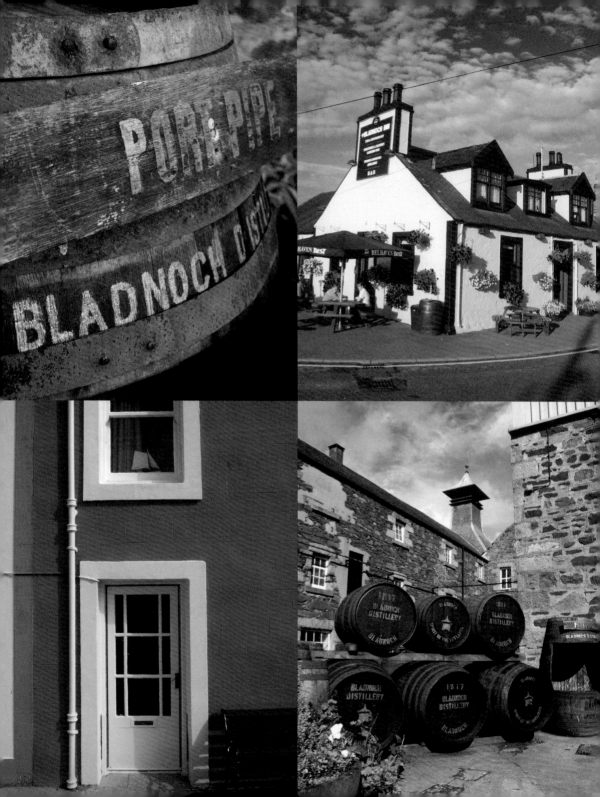

marthrown of mabie

Huddled around a life-preserving fire that illuminated the gloom of their Iron Age roundhouse, our ancestors eked out a living in places like Mabie Forest. Today you can follow in their footsteps in what has to be one of Europe's first reconstructed Iron Age roundhouses that you can actually stay the night in. Get down and dirty and all elemental whilst cooking your own food over the crackling fire, enjoying the pleasures of an al-fresco toilet and a dense and moody forest where little has changed over the last few millennia.

Marthrown is a special place in so many ways. The forest itself is awash with native Caledonian trees, with characterful old Scots pines each managing the wilful Scottish trick of being a different shape to the rest of their brood, as well as birch, rowan and juniper. Edging over the grassy mound that separates the heart of the 'multi-activity centre' from the roundhouse, you half expect to find a gaggle of hunter-gatherers crowded around a clearing where once Celtic songs and stories were celebrated in wild ceilidhs.

Today, the roundhouse – an impressive construction that manages to stand up to the full might of the Atlantic weather

systems sweeping in off the coast – is similarly full of life. Perfect for groups, as it sleeps 16, it inevitably plays host to the occasional stag and hen party, and is also popular with groups of friends looking for something a bit different. And different it is: you camp around the central fire whilst smoke fills the air and then rises out through the roof, which helpfully also keeps the rain out. Just nearby is a canvas tipi that sleeps an additional eight people, though the roundhouse is the real star. Tents are also welcome and it is possible to hire the whole site for exclusive use.

Rather than just sticking up the roundhouse and leaving it at that, the family team behind Marthrown have made an effort to re-create other earthy features, which fit neatly into today's vogue for all things clean and green. Rather than clog the local sewage system there is a simple but highly effective odour-free straw urinal as well as a composting 'flush' toilet. Luxurious extras include a sauna and hot pool that are free for guests.

The surrounding forest, which is alive with red squirrels and woodpeckers, is one of the best locations in Scotland for mountain biking. You can hire a bike on site from the dedicated cycle centre and explore the forest, which has recently been opened up as part of the excellent 'Seven Stanes' programme. All skill levels are catered for, with everything from easy and gently undulating forest trails that are perfect for beginners to some seriously testing 'black runs' that fling you at high speed down through tough terrain with vaulting trees on either side.

At Marthrown itself there are two 12-metre climbing towers that offer low and high

ropes, as well as the epic 'Leap of Faith' which has sorted the men from the boys on many a stag weekend. However you spend your day at Marthrown, the highlight is getting back around that fire. Whether you are in one big group or just sharing space with complete strangers there is a real sense of community and of getting back to basics. Taking a starlit stroll and then walking back to the welcoming and gently smoking arms of the simple dwelling is a strangely comforting experience that people have been enjoying for thousands of years.

THE UPSIDE: Enjoy the simple life like your ancestors and cosy nights by the fire.

THE DOWNSIDE: The extra £5 charge for campers to use the kitchen facilities.

THE DAMAGE: £12.50 per person in the roundhouse; 1–3-person tents £10; hired tents £20.

THE FACILITIES: Hot showers, a kitchen, sauna and hot pool. You can also get breakfast for £3.50 and 3-course dinners for £8.

NEAREST DECENT PUB: You will be spoilt for choice in Dumfries 5 miles away. One of the best

is the riverside Coach and Horses (01387 256224), which serves hearty pub grub.

IF IT RAINS: Stay in and stoke up a fire, or visit the nearby town of Dumfries.

GETTING THERE: Leave Dumfries on the A710 towards New Abbey. When you reach Islesteps look out for the right turn to Mabie Forest and Mabie House Hotel. When you come to the sign for Mabie House Hotel the road bears left and you will see signs for Marthrown of Mabie Education Centre. The site is a mile from here along a forest track.

PUBLIC TRANSPORT: Buses run by MacEwan's Coach Services (01387 256533) operate from Dumfries to Cargenbridge. From here you can walk to Marthrown of Mabie, but it will take around 45 minutes.

OPEN: All year.

IF IT'S FULL: No roundhouse alternatives nearby, but Kirk Loch Caravan and Camping Site (01556 502521), 12 miles away to the northeast, occupies a great spot on the shores of Lochmaben.

| **Marthrown of Mabie**, Mabie Forest, Dumfries DG2 8HB | t | 01387 247900 | w | www.marthrown.com |

beecraigs country park

If you think that a country park in provincial West Lothian is an unlikely place for a cool campsite then you are in for a pleasant surprise. Just 20 miles from Edinburgh and 35 miles from Glasgow is a site as handy as you can get for Scotland's two biggest cities – and you can also get here by bike along an old canal path from both. Beecraigs Country Park itself is shrouded with trees, has its own loch and a nearby prehistoric site with perhaps the finest view in Central Scotland, as well as being right by one of the nation's most important historic towns.

The town of Linlithgow, the birthplace of the formidable Mary Queen of Scots, is well worth visiting. Its centrepiece is Mary's ruined 16th-century palace and the equally impressive medieval church of St Michael's, whose tower is topped by a controversial modern addition, a metal crown that resembles silver swords stretching up to puncture the heavens. If after touring the town's niche shops, old world tearooms and nefarious hostelries – the cobbled High Street has no fewer than eight pubs – you can escape with a stroll around Linlithgow Loch. The walk takes around an hour and, provided you can avoid the army of scavenging swans, opens up a great view of the palace.

You don't, however, really need to leave Beecraigs Country Park. Located right at the heart of the park, the small campsite nestles among towering pine trees and during the week you may well have it all to yourself; we did in early September. Picnic benches and barbecues are also on hand, so if you've forgotten to bring your burgers then make a beeline for the farm shop at the Park Centre, where you can buy plump venison steaks. (If you're a sensitive soul, perhaps you should avoid a walk around their deer farm afterwards.)

Nestled amongst the undulating Bathgate Hills, the park feels a million miles from the rest of bustling Central Scotland. It boasts forest trails for walkers and bikers and a freshwater loch where, if you buy a permit, you can row out on a small boat, cast your line and wait patiently for a bite. You can also keep fit on the 'trim course' or book an activity course (archery, canoeing, climbing, abseiling, kayaking and orienteering) with the park's Outdoor Activity Centre; the climbing wall and the archery course are available for exclusive use by the hour.

If you're camping with children, or even if you're not, the deer farm and fishery also appeal. At the deer farm you can watch stately red stags and pregnant or nursing does from an elevated platform or join a guided walk. At the fishery the rainbow trout that find their way into the loch each day are kept in large holding tanks, where you can watch the fish whip themselves up into a frenzy when they are fed. You can also buy some seriously fresh trout to cook back at the campsite.

With so much going on at the park you could be forgiven for leaving without having visited the area's main attraction – Cairnpapple. This ancient burial mound is one of the nation's most important prehistoric monuments and, handily, it offers perhaps the finest views of any wee hill in Central Scotland. From the top of the cairn you can take in everything from the mighty rock 'sisters' of Ailsa Craig in the west to Bass Rock in the east. Don't worry about the sign that displays the official opening times – these refer only to the reconstructed cairn and, if it's closed when you arrive, you can still climb up to witness the views that will immediately blast you away.

THE UPSIDE: Criminally undiscovered by most tourists; caravans are parked in various 'groves' away from the tents.

THE DOWNSIDE: Public transport is pretty non-existent.

THE DAMAGE: Fees depend on the size of your tent and season and range from £7 for a single-berth tent to £16 for a large tent.

THE FACILITIES: Heated toilet block, hot showers, launderette, dishwashing room, public telephone and barbecues.

NEAREST DECENT PUB: In nearby Linlithgow, you're spoilt for choice. The pick of the bunch is The Four Marys (01506 842171). There's also an exceptional eatery nearby, the Bruntonside Restaurant (01506 652133; www.bruntonside.co.uk), which is located just 4 miles from the campsite at Torpichen and is acclaimed for its fresh local ingredients and extensive wine list.

IF IT RAINS: Take a cruise on the Union Canal. The Linlithgow Union Canal Society (01506 671215) run trips from Easter to October, with daily trips in July and August. Or enjoy a lazy lunch at Bruntonside (see above).

GETTING THERE: Leave the M9 at junction 4 if you're travelling from the west or junction 3 if you're travelling from the east. Then follow the A803 into Linlithgow, from there you'll pick up signs to the campsite.

PUBLIC TRANSPORT: You'll need to catch either the train (08457 484950) or the bus to Linlithgow and then hike there or grab a taxi. First Edinburgh (08708 727271) run buses to Linlithgow from Edinburgh, Stirling and Falkirk.

OPEN: Apr–Oct.

IF IT'S FULL: Another handy option for exploring Edinburgh is Linwater Caravan Park (0131 3333326; www.linwater.co.uk), 11 miles west of Edinburgh, which has a sheltered, tents-only area. It's signposted off the B7030.

Beecraigs Country Park Campsite, Near Linlithgow, West Lothian EH49 6PL | t | 01506 844518 | w | www.beecraigs.com

mains farm

If you've always dreamed of running through the glens like a badly face-painted Mel Gibson yelling 'Freedom!', fancied yourself as a champion of the poor or just feel you could ham up a better Scottish accent than Liam Neeson in *Rob Roy*, then Mains Farm campsite is the perfect location. You don't need a fertile imagination to relax and unwind amidst the Lowland scenery that was once the stomping ground of William 'Braveheart' Wallace and Scotland's very own Robin Hood, Rob Roy MacGregor.

Located on the eastern fringes of Thornhill, the campsite is ideal for those who want the convenience of village amenities without sacrificing a remote location. It also offers campers three distinct options: sleep under canvas, retreat to the comfort of a heated wooden wigwam or snooze like Hiawatha inside a giant tipi. Constructed in a traditional Sioux design and handmade in the Scottish Borders, the striking red, white and blue canvas tipi was only the second of its kind when it opened for business in 2006. It's worth the £50 fee for the novelty alone but is great for families and small groups looking for something different.

If your attempts at holding a pow wow and living like an Indian squaw are dashed because the tipi is fully booked, then pitching in the spacious field across the road is the best option (the wigwams are quite closely packed together). Even if all 34 camping pitches are occupied, and they rarely are, you will still have plenty of room. One of the best things about the campsite is its open views over the Carse of Stirling and the Fintry Hills, but it is also mighty close to the historic city of Stirling, whose castle is one of Scotland's most alluring.

The Fintry Hills offer some fine low-level walking as well as the chance to follow in the footsteps of the Scottish outlaw Rob Roy, who roamed the area more than three centuries ago. For his peers, passing judgement on MacGregor was easy: his enemies dubbed him a thief and racketeer, whilst the poor people he helped along the way hailed him as a hero. Today, the legend of Rob Roy is symbolic of the systematic destruction of the clan way of life, with the once-wealthy MacGregor family hounded off their land and relentlessly persecuted by lowland Scots loyal to the English king.

The Wallace Monument, located just outside Stirling, is also evocative of centuries of injustice and a lasting testimony to an even more famous Scot, Sir William Wallace, who was born 400 years before Rob Roy. Although Mel Gibson's Hollywood depiction of the great Scots warrior had cannonball-sized historical holes and the actor's stature was woefully short (the real Wallace was a giant), the 1995 *Braveheart* film still compels people to visit Stirling.

The towering monument was built in 1869 to symbolise Wallace's biggest victory at the Battle of Stirling Bridge. Standing defiantly atop Abbey Craig, the monument marks the vantage point from where Wallace watched the English advance before leading a blood-bath that claimed the lives of more than 5,000 English soldiers with the loss of only a few hundred Scots. Inside the museum you can see the warrior's merciless sword, which measures a staggering 1.64 metres.

If you are a film buff, avid historian or just an incurably romantic soul then the myths and legends of this part of the world are an irresistible draw. If you've seen the film, bought the DVD and got the T-shirt, perhaps it's time you visited the campsite.

UPSIDE: Great base for exploring William Wallace and Rob Roy country.

DOWNSIDE: Fairly basic amenities.

THE DAMAGE: £4.50 per tent, £1.75 per adult and 75p per child.

THE FACILITIES: Toilets, hot showers, electric hook-ups. Those staying in wigwams or the tipi have access to a kitchen.

NEAREST DECENT PUB: Just 5 minutes from the campsite the Lion and Unicorn (01786 850204) is a reasonable option. For one of the best dining experiences in the region make the 4-mile journey to the Inn at Kippen gastropub (01786 871010), where traditional Scottish dishes like salmon, beef and chicken are spiced with Mediterranean and Asian influences.

IF IT RAINS: Seize the opportunity to wander around Stirling's 15th and 16th century castle. If the rain clears, you will also get sweeping views from atop this craggy extinct volcano.

GETTING THERE: From the M9 follow the signs to the A84 Callandar. From the A84 turn left onto the A837, which becomes Thornhill's Main Street. Turn left onto the B822 and the campsite is on your left.

PUBLIC TRANSPORT: First Edinburgh (01324 602200) buses run from Stirling to Thornhill.

OPEN: Easter–Oct (campsite), Mar–Nov (wigwams and tipi).

IF IT'S FULL: The well-maintained Auchenbowie Caravan Site (01324 822141) is located just 14 miles away and 4 miles outside of Stirling. You're likely to find more caravans here, but tents are welcome.

Mains Farm, Kippen Road, Thornhill FK8 3QB	t	01786 850605 (campsite), 01786 850735 (wigwams and tipi)
	w	www.mainsfarmwigwams.com (wigwams and tipi)

easter drumquhassle farm

At a time when many farms are turning their backs on traditional farming in favour of more lucrative options like converting to farmstead housing or luxury flats, Easter Drumquhassle Farm makes a refreshing change. The animals around here are not just for show, with sheep being grazed as the main farming activity with horses also at livery at this 40-acre site. Making your way to the shower in the morning, you have as much chance of running into a charging duck or clucking hen as you do a fellow camper.

As well as farming and camping, there's also a cosy B&B in one of the 19th-century farm buildings, a cosy escape on a wet day. Most of the campers arriving here, however, are just happy to find anywhere to crash – Easter Drumquhassle Farm is a stopping point on the epic walk of the West Highland Way.

The West Highland Way, which runs past the campsite, is Scotland's most famous long-distance walk. Easter Drumquhassle Farm is a virtually obligatory stop for walkers, because, as a sign at the entrance so proudly points out: 'This is the only campsite in the Drymen area'. You can usually tell which way

walkers have come, as those heading north from Glasgow will be nursing just a few first-day blisters and tweaks, while those staggering in from the north will have a catalogue of aches and pains, and more than a few tall stories after trekking all the way from Fort William.

The site is spread across a small grassy field, dotted with trees, which provide some shelter, but the ground can be quite hard in places, so bring a mallet and watch out for roots when pitching. The views are expansive, with rolling fields all around and the Kilpatrick Hills rising in the distance. The site itself offers a few creature comforts – the shower and toilet facilities are basic, but there is a rudimentary wet-weather shelter in an old barn and there are also two heated wigwams for those looking for a step up in luxury. The owners also offer the option of a cooked breakfast in the morning, a nourishing extra welcomed by many walkers.

Even for those not enthused by long walks, a quick stroll on the West Highland Way is practically compulsory at Drumquhassle. An easy option is to trek up the road a couple of

miles north to the small town of Drymen, where a sprinkling of welcoming pubs brighten up the main square. The site owners offer lifts to and from the pub for the terminally lazy, through the walk is lovely on a balmy evening, slipping past fields with glimpses of Loch Lomond on one flank and the Campsie Fells on the other.

The name Drumquhassle comes from the Gaelic 'drum', meaning ridge, with the 'quhassle' referring to the Roman Fort on the hill near the campsite. The site has yet to be excavated, but you can troop up and take a look at the place where it stood marking the northern boundary of the Roman Empire.

Easter Drumquhassle will never win awards for its range of facilities, but if you're looking for an honest, relaxed site where you can kick back and watch the world go by, or launch yourself onto the West Highland Way, then it fits the bill. You cannot fail to love a place where the only real downside is being woken up in the morning by an over-eager cockerel – and even that can be forgiven when you tuck into a hearty cooked breakfast with free-range eggs in the old farmhouse.

THE UPSIDE: Real farm feel and hearty cooked breakfasts that set you up for the day.

THE DOWNSIDE: Facilities on the very basic side of adequate.

THE DAMAGE: Tent £4 per night; wigwam £7 per night; whole wigwam £32. B&B £19–25 per person per night.

THE FACILITIES: Wet-weather shelter with a small kitchen area, toilets and hot shower.

NEAREST DECENT PUB: The historic Clachan Inn (01360 660824) in Drymen, dating back to 1734, is just less than 2 miles away and serves up reliable pub grub and some excellent Scottish ales including Belhaven Best.

IF IT RAINS: The wet-weather shelter provides some respite, whilst the visitor centre complex at Loch Lomond Shores (www.lochlomondshores.com) and the buzzing city of Glasgow are both an easy drive away.

GETTING THERE: The campsite is a 30-minute drive from Stirling. Take the A811 west for 20 miles and then look out for a turn towards Gartness. The site is along the old Gartness Road and is signposted.

PUBLIC TRANSPORT: There is no direct public transport to the site, though trains run from Glasgow Queen Street to Alexandria (08457 484950), where you can connect with a local bus to Drymen run by McColl's Coaches (01389 754321).

OPEN: All year.

IF IT'S FULL: Other Cool Camping sites at Beinglas (p51), at the other end of Loch Lomond, and Luss (p45) are not too far away. Alternatively 'wild' camp by the shores of Loch Lomond in the marked site at the foot of the mountain at Rowardennan (no facilities).

Easter Drumquhassle Farm, Gartness Road, Drymen, By Loch Lomond G63 0DN

| | t | 01360 660893 | w | http://members.aol.com/juliamacx |

luss

It is no wonder that campers and caravaners alike are attracted to the famously 'bonnie, bonnie banks' of Loch Lomond. Great Britain's largest stretch of freshwater lies just north of Glasgow in a shroud of mountains, peppered with little islands and fringed by a phalanx of trees. The problem is that some of the campsites on and around the loch cater to the lowest common denominator, packing in caravans and, as an afterthought, squeezing in tents too. At Luss, however, campers are treated as well as those with hulking motor homes and actually enjoy some of the best spots right by the water's edge.

Loch Lomond, together with the adjacent Trossach Hills, is now part of a protected national park – the existing caravan parks along this shoreline were approved before the park came into existence. Whilst the caravans and campervans have to make do with those spots set back from the loch, tenters get the million-dollar views at the water's edge.

Beyond the little stony beach, the loch stretches into the distance whilst in the background looms Ben Lomond and its Ptarmigan Ridge. (The route along the Ptarmigan Ridge is more interesting and rewarding than that taken by most tourists, although it is steep and can be tricky in poor weather.)

Unlike many of Scotland's rough and ready campsites, Luss is as prim and proper as a good Highland B&B. The tone is set by the amenity block, which is housed in a trim, stonewashed old house. Toilets and showers are spotless and there is even fresh lavender in the washing room. The on-site shop sells Avon Skin So Soft, which is nigh on essential for keeping the fierce midges away in summer. For kids there is a playground with swings as well as a parent and child room.

The name of the site comes from the nearby village of Luss, easily the prettiest village in these parts, which you can walk to from the campsite. On arrival, don't be surprised if the village looks surreally familiar – it was the star of the Scottish soap opera *Take the High Road*. You can see why the producers chose the site as the slate-workers' cottages, the quaint village church and the loch-view main street are all postcard-perfect.

Today, Luss is a great place to relax for a morning; it's worth coming early, though, before the tour buses arrive in summer. There are a couple of laid-back little cafés offering home baking and heart-starting soup, a variety of souvenir shops for stocking up on trinkets and also a boat pier. At the pier, you'll find loch tours on offer – these are a great way to appreciate the sheer scale of this vast body of water and some of its myriad islands.

There is no doubt that Loch Lomond well deserves its popularity, which is why the hotels in this area are predominantly overpriced, and most of the campsites cater for the caravan market. Thankfully, Luss Caravan and Camping Club Site offers campers the chance to secure a prime loch-side pitch – and for once beat the caravans for the best views.

THE UPSIDE: Those loch views; get as close as you can.

THE DOWNSIDE: The busy A82 runs nearby, though depending on the wind, the noise is not usually a major problem.

THE DAMAGE: Up to £7.25 per person in summer.

THE FACILITIES: Good, with on-site shop, modern and spotless toilet, shower and washing block.

NEAREST DECENT PUB: Just north of the village of Luss is the 200-year-old Inverbeg Inn (01436 860678). This cosy and welcoming place offers bar food, more sophisticated meals and a good selection of draught ales.

IF IT RAINS: Loch Lomond Shores (www.lochlomondshores.com) visitor centre lies at the southern end of the loch offering films, exhibits and boat trips. There's also an array of shops and plenty of places to eat and drink.

GETTING THERE: From Glasgow simply follow the A82 north through Dumbarton. The road hits the loch at Balloch and continues up the western flank before reaching the village of Luss. The campsite itself is just north of the village off the A82.

PUBLIC TRANSPORT: Scottish Citylink buses (08705 505050) from Glasgow pass by the site.

OPEN: Mar–Oct.

IF IT'S FULL: Nearby sites include Beinglas (p51) and Easter Drumquhassle Farm (p39).

Luss Camping and Caravanning Site, Luss, Loch Lomond, Nr Glasgow G83 8NT				
	t	01436 860658	w	www.campingandcaravanningclub.co.uk

beinglas farm

You don't *have* to don a pair of sturdy boots caked in mud and an impressive, branded, hi-tech waterproof jacket, but they will certainly help you fit in at Beinglas. The site is located in ridiculously sublime scenery, just north of Britain's largest stretch of freshwater at Loch Lomond and is surrounded by brooding mountain peaks. It's pure walkers heaven – but that doesn't mean there's no appeal for other visitors too.

The road access itself is almost designed to put off non-walkers, a nerve-defying sharp right turn when heading north across the busy A82, and then over a bumpy bridge. A much better way to enter Beinglas is on the famous West Highland Way long-distance walk, with the campsite lying in Glenfalloch 25 miles north of the southern start of the trail at Milngavie. Arrive early, whether you're walking or not, because although the large field that houses the site may hold up to 100 tents it can fill up and the best spots go quickly in summer.

If taking on a stretch of the West Highland Way does not tempt you then there are numerous other hills and mountains nearby.

The peak that gives the site its name, Ben Glas, is dramatic in its own right, rising just behind the site. The mountain that acts as a magnet for walkers from all over, though, is Ben Lomond. One of the Munro mountains, Ben Lomond makes an excellent starting climb (five to six hours up and down, with the 'tourist path' as easy as they come; though the usual mountain precautions apply). From the top of Ben Lomond you may well be bitten by the Munro-bagging bug as you can see a fair few of them from there, though the thought that you still have another 283 mountains over 900 metres to go is quite a sobering one.

Whilst the A82 is enough to put off even the most hardened of city cyclists, the countryside around Beinglas is perfect for touring by car. There are distilleries, visitor centres and what seems like yet another loch at every turn; Loch Lomond is just two miles south of the campsite. If you are into seafood then the charms of the original Loch Fyne Seafood Restaurant (01499 600236; www.lochfyne.com) are less than an hour's drive away by the banks of the eponymous loch.

Back at the site, the social hub is the large amenity block that comes complete with a shop dishing out maps, first-aid kits and other walking paraphernalia, as well as an impressive wet-weather shelter that boasts a pool table, laundrette, pay phone, seating and cookers. There is also a bar, popular in the evenings with outdoor types recalling the day's adventures. It also has live bands at weekends. In summer, the beer garden outside is the place to sit and enjoy a pint as the sun sets behind the craggy peaks.

If the weather turns, there are four wigwams on site, two large and two small, tucked at the back of the camp under the watchful eye of Ben Glas. These provide the perfect sanctuary after a day in the hills, but if you want to fit in you might as well pitch in with the rest of the West Highland Way devotees and join in the fun down on the camping field no matter how wild it gets. When you have walked so far to get here, you'll sleep well in any weather.

THE UPSIDE: A paradise for walkers with the West Highland Way running right through the site and great scenery.

THE DOWNSIDE: Truly treacherous turn for drivers heading north.

THE DAMAGE: Camping costs £6 per person; wigwams £12 per person.

THE FACILITIES: Hot showers, shop, bar serving food and wet-weather shelter with cooking facilities and a pool table.

NEAREST DECENT PUB: Stay on-site or head a little further afield to the famous Drovers Inn (01301 704234; www.thedroversinn.co.uk) in the same village of Inverarnan, where you'll find a surreal mix of tatty taxidermy, centuries-old interior design and kilt-sporting barmen.

IF IT RAINS: Make new friends and enjoy good food and Scottish ale in the on-site lounge bar and restaurant until the weather improves. Or unwind over a few rounds of pool in the camping shelter.

GETTING THERE: Simply follow the A82 from Glasgow north towards Loch Lomond. The road cuts around the western flank; continue past the village of Luss and the campsite is signposted on the right with that horrible turn taking you across a small bridge into the site.

PUBLIC TRANSPORT: Citylink (08705 505050) buses ply the A82 every day from Glasgow.

OPEN: All year, except Christmas.

IF IT'S FULL: Try the Cool Camping sites at Easter Drumquhassle Farm (p39) and Luss (p45).

Beinglas Farm Campsite, Inverarnan, Loch Lomond, Dumbartonshire G83 7DX

| | t | 01301 704281 | w | www.beinglascampsite.co.uk |

strathfillan wigwams

It is a wonderful feeling on a horrible *dreich* (you don't need to be Scottish to work out what this wonderful slice of Scots onomatopoeia means) day. You have spent hours trudging through the torrential rain, your waterproofs have long since wimped out, your feet are chronically blistered and all you have to look forward to is struggling your tent up in the deluge. Then it happens: you discover the campsite has heated wooden wigwams, little oases of dryness where you can wring out your clothes, warm up your extremities and kick back with a hot drink. This is the feeling that greets walkers on the West Highland Way at Strathfillan and it is a feeling you can also enjoy without having to do the hard bit first.

Strathfillan sits right on the West Highland Way long-distance walking trail in a pass that cuts through the surrounding stadium of mountains. It's just east of the world famous West Highland Railway, which also ekes through the testing high ground here. The site tumbles down from the railway line on a tree-shrouded hillside with the wigwams dotted around the greenery. Tents can be pitched either near the wigwams on a flat grassy plain by the entrance or just across the West Highland Way in a small soft grassy field that enjoys the best views.

The Indian theme extends beyond the wigwams (which come in two sizes: standard and plus) with the 'Trading Post' shop on site looking like something out of a West End theatre version of the Wild West. Inside you can stock up on such essentials as Indian headgear, Native American crafts and a range of cuddly toys. Strathfillan is nothing if not eclectic with the exoticisms of beef jerky and emu burgers backed up by more standard comfort food like dried pasta and pasta sauces in jars.

Even if you don't consider yourself a walker, it is hard, on a sky-splittingly blue summer day, to resist the urge to meander along the West Highland Way, at least for a little while as it teases off into the mountains. If this stirs your appetite for more arduous exercise then a number of walking trails passing through woodland, waterfalls and lush farmland, leave from the campsite. Details are available from the campsite reception and are also posted on a map in

TAXI
AVAILABLE
ON
SITE
07866897230
OSTRICH FEATHER
£4 £6 £8 DUSTERS
OSTRICH EGGS
£6·75
CHILDREN'S
MOOD RING

the kitchen of the wigwam facility block. If you want to set yourself a challenge on an altogether different scale, then set off to 'bag' one of the many Munros (mountains with peaks more than 900 metres above sea level) in the area.

Of course, you may prefer to explore the surrounding countryside by car or bicycle. The area is dotted with lochs, but perhaps the finest is Loch Lubnaig, a personal favourite of the *Cool Camping* team. It may not actually be in the Highlands, but this slip of freshwater sits proudly at the foot of mighty Ben Shian in the midst of the thick Strathyre Forest. There is a parking spot where you can enjoy a picnic and even pop

in for a swim when the mercury gets up; though, there is also the option of taking out a canoe.

It may boast wigwams and Indian feather headgear, but Strathfillan is still wonderfully Scottish. It has its tongue firmly in its cheek and lies in the sort of swathe of scenery that actually makes postcards worth buying. Getting drenched and testing yourself against the elements remains a very enjoyable Scottish pastime, but the beauty of Strathfillan is that you can enjoy a slice of Calvinist punishment before having the option of retreating to the luxury of your enjoyably comfortable heated wigwam shelter.

THE UPSIDE: Wigwams on hand when it rains in a picturesque location right on the West Highland Way.

THE DOWNSIDE: Endless walking tales from your fellow campers if you pitch a tent here.

THE DAMAGE: Camping costs £5 per adult and £2.50 per child; wigwams cost £11–12.50 per adult and £7–8 per child.

THE FACILITIES: Decent toilet blocks with hot showers, fully equipped kitchens, TV lounge/dining room, drying room, washing machine, tumble dryer and Trading Post shop.

NEAREST DECENT PUB: The Real Food Café (www.therealfoodcafe.com) in Tyndrum is the place to head for award winning local ales, home baking, tempura and 100% local beef burgers from the farm at Strathfillan Wigwams.

IF IT RAINS: Take a ride on the scenic West Highland Railway (08457 484950) from Crianlarich.

GETTING THERE: From Stirling take the A82 north through Crianlarich towards Tyndrum. The site is just off to the right before you arrive in the village of Tyndrum itself.

PUBLIC TRANSPORT: Scottish Citylink (0870 505050) services from Glasgow stop at Tyndrum on route to the Isle of Skye.

OPEN: All year.

IF IT'S FULL: Fellow *Cool Camping* site Beinglas (p51) is to the south or continue north to Glen Etive for wild camping (p216).

Strathfillan Wigwams, Auchtertyre, Tyndrum, Crianlarich FK20 8RU

| | t | 01838 400251 | w | www.sac.ac.uk/wigwams |

loch tay highland lodges

There may be a trio of campsites dotted in quick succession along the western shores of Loch Tay, but only one of them has its own on-site equestrian centre. And a marina with the largest teaching fleet of open-keel sailing dinghies in Scotland, a flotilla of Canadian canoes and plenty of other watersports opportunities. And a bar and restaurant with waterfront terrace. You certainly won't be short of things to do at Loch Tay.

Loch Tay Highland Lodges sit right on the loch spread across a 140-acre estate, most of which is occupied by holiday-park-style wooden lodges, but there's also a small campsite – tucked away, back up the hill overlooking the equestrian centre and the loch, a safe distance from the wooden lodges. As well as half a dozen tent pitches there are also six heated wooden tipis on the campsite, green-painted pyramids that look quite organic and low-impact from the outside, but with interiors styled on a cheap B&B. They come as either 'standard' with TVs and fridges, or 'standard plus' with their own kitchenettes and showers.

Whether you stay in a tent or attempt to seek refuge from the midges in a tipi, you'll probably spend most of your time outdoors anyway, with all that's on offer. Water-based options include learning to sail on the loch, hiring a sailing dinghy or joining an organised kayak trip to the village of Killin, where a minibus will pick you up to save the effort of paddling back against the wind. You can also rent a boat and buy a fishing permit in order to bring back some nice, juicy salmon or trout for dinner.

On land, a fleet of mountain and hybrid bikes await, with organised trips around the surrounding countryside. Adrenaline junkies will jump at the chance to be dropped off in the hills to return via speedy downhills on a 20-mile thrill ride. For those seeking a slower pace, you can also hire tandem hybrid bikes and children's bicycles. Then, there is the 18-hole putting green, an archery range and clay-pigeon shooting, allowing you to savour the experience of blowing up clays over the silvery waters of Loch Tay. The Equestrian Centre (01567 820736) is also open all year and trekking, hacking and tuition are all available, so bring your jodhpurs.

One of the main attractions of this region, though, doesn't cost a penny and is what lures most people here – the panorama of rugged mountains and shimmering lochs that vault all around. Climbers and walkers will want to head up the slopes of Ben Lawers, a monster of a mountain at about 1350 metres, whose summit affords stunning views of numerous Scottish peaks and Loch Tay stretching out its tentacles far below.

If all these action-packed activities leave you in need of something a touch more pedestrian, then a visit to the village of Fortingall will reveal the oldest yew tree in Europe, believed to be between 3,000 and 5,000 years old. Although the tree predates the adjacent church by millennia, it is fitting that a house of prayer should have been erected there, with yew trees traditionally associated with religious worship. Sadly, the authorities were forced to construct a protective wall around the yew to prevent tourists from snipping off twigs and branches.

Whether it is marvelling at ancient trees, crashing downhill on a mountain bike, having your first go at sailing or taking on a few jumps on a horse, Loch Tay has it all. But none of these activities would be here if Loch Tay wasn't a gloriously beautiful place to visit in its own right. And that can be appreciated with the minimum of effort – just a few leisurely steps from your tent.

THE UPSIDE: There is enough to keep you occupied for a week, both in the water and out.

THE DOWNSIDE: Poor toilet block and a few too many lodges dotted around the hillside.

THE DAMAGE: £8.50 per 2-person tent then £2 extra per adult. The wooden tipis cost £12–14 per person in bunks, and sleep up to 4. Each tipi also has a meter for electricity.

THE FACILITIES: There's a toilet and shower block nearby, which needs to be refurbished, though you can use the new facilities at the marina without charge.

NEAREST DECENT PUB: The on-site Boat House (01567 820853) was purpose-built to take advantage of the loch views with a wooden deck overlooking the marina. It serves bar meals, pizza and pre-ordered packed lunches.

IF IT RAINS: Make the journey to the other side of the loch to the Ardeonaig Hotel & Restaurant (01567 820400) to enjoy the finest burgers in this part of Scotland as well as huge steaks.

GETTING THERE: From the M9 take the A84 to Callander. Continue north from Lochearnhead on the A85 before turning right on the A827 to Killin.

Continue through the village and the campsite is signposted to the right after a couple of miles.

PUBLIC TRANSPORT: Caber Coaches (01887 820090) operate a bus service from Aberfeldy to Morenish. The campsite is 10 minutes' walk from the Morenish bus stop.

OPEN: All year.

IF IT'S FULL: The lodges can be booked for a minimum of 2 nights. Cruachan Farm (01567 820302) is just a stone's throw west on the road back to Killin.

Loch Tay Highland Lodges, Milton Morenish Estate, by Killin, Perthshire FK21 8TY

| | t | 01567 820323 | w | www.lochtay-vacations.co.uk |

glengoulandie

On arrival at Glengoulandie Campsite, you'll probably be greeted by Leanne Wright with the sort of welcome you only get at a small, family-owned site. This warmest of welcomes might be because she spends her days surrounded by deer rather than people. But, set amidst the rolling hills and cobalt blue lochs of Perthshire and in the shadow of one of Scotland's most striking mountains – the legendary Schiehallion – this semi-solitary location has an obvious, scenic upside.

The site at Glengoulandie nestles at the foot of another hill – Dùn Coillich – and is fringed by a trickling burn and deer farm. If you're camping you can easily turn your back on the static caravans at the rear of the site and when the campsite is busy Leanne is sensitive enough to try to pitch families and walkers separately. Leanne's hands-on approach reflects the pride that she takes in the campsite; a pride that has fuelled Glengoulandie's environmentally minded ethos. Only eco-friendly products are used at the site, and she also operates a bio-sewage system and recycles as much waste as possible.

Within the campsite, there is plenty to keep you occupied, with an on-site shop and café, deer farm (campers can walk around here free of charge, but a more fun alternative is to hire the park's 4x4 and go for a spin) and a modest-sized fishing lochan (small lake) brimming with rainbow trout. According to Leanne the Land Registry department asked them what they wanted to call their lake, so they are hoping that Loch Coillich will soon appear on official maps. In the shop you can also buy postcards of the park's Highland cows (those cute furry ones), deer, ducks, peacocks (which used to roam around the campsite until they started pecking people's cars) and chickens. The postcards have been reproduced from photographs that Leanne, a budding snapper, took herself.

Walkers are lured to the campsite by Schiehallion, the 'Fairy Hill of the Caledonians', a hulking and threatening-looking conical mountain that towers to 1083 metres. Despite an ascent that is both steep and tiring, this is one of the easiest and most rewarding Munro ascents for those properly equipped. Schiehallion's location also cuts down on the travelling time for

'Munro baggers', the mad souls determined to summit all of Scotland's 284 peaks over 900 metres high before they die. The main path starts at the Braes of Foss car park. You can try to summit from the campsite but Leanne warns against the overgrown route.

On a clear day atop Schiehallion, all the 'feels like you are on top of the world' clichés ring true. You can see Loch Rannoch, Rannoch Moor, Loch Tummel and the lower hills of the Central Highlands. If you have no interest in tackling Schiehallion, it is notable for another reason. In the 18th century, the Astronomer-Royal hiked up the mountain in a bid to learn about the earth's mass; an expedition that was central to the development of map contours. So in some respects, the maps we all use today owe a great debt to Schiehallion.

Dùn Coillich itself is also unique. The 1,100-acre hill has been owned by the Highland Perthshire Communities Land Trust since January 2002 as a result of the first successful community land buy-out in the region. You can ramble around the hill, looking out for the 70 bird species, including golden eagles, and see the fledgling restoration of the rowan, birch and willow forest, with the first of 30,000 saplings planted at the end of 2005. This is exactly the sort of sustainable approach that Leanne Wright and most visitors to Glengoulandie approve of.

THE UPSIDE: Camp amongst the hills and mountains of Perthshire and share a site with deer.

THE DOWNSIDE: Home to around two dozen static caravans.

THE DAMAGE: Fees depend on the size of your tent and range from £8 for a 1–2-person tent to £14 for an 8–10-person tent.

THE FACILITIES: Laundry, café, shop, hot showers and toilets.

NEAREST DECENT PUB: It's a long walk (7 miles) to the nearest decent pub, the Ailean Chraggan (01887 820346), which is located on the road towards Aberfeldy in Weem. You'll be rewarded with innovative fish and game dishes, as well as views over Loch Tay.

IF IT RAINS: Head for Dewar's World of Whisky (01887 822010) in Aberfeldy and learn about whisky on the distillery tour, or invest in a 12-year-old Aberfeldy single malt.

GETTING THERE: Heading north from Edinburgh on the M90/A9 towards Inverness, take the A827 towards Aberfeldy and then the B846 towards Kinloch Rannoch; the campsite is 8 or 9 miles along this road.

PUBLIC TRANSPORT: Stagecoach Perth (01738 629339) run buses from Perth to Aberfeldy. The Broons Buses and Taxis (01882 632331) service from Aberfeldy to Kinloch Rannoch goes past the campsite.

OPEN: Mar–Oct.

IF IT'S FULL: Other good campsites in the region include Ardgualich Farm (p75) or the SCA Campsite at Grandtully (p69).

Glengoulandie Campsite, Glengoulandie Country Park, by Pitlochry, Perthshire PH16 5NL

| t | 01887 830495 | w | www.glengoulandie.co.uk |

scottish canoe association grandtully campsite

Bouncing over whitewater rapids on an inflatable raft, screaming for your life as water sprays in your face and soaks through to your skin is one sure way to kick out your stress at the end of a busy week. And if you're staying at the Grandtully campsite, then exhilarating rafting is right on your doorstep.

It is not just the campsite's location, set back around 100 metres from the thundering River Tay, that makes it a good base. Unlike the other more commercial sites in the area (which are largely geared towards touring caravans), the campsite has space for a maximum of 50 tents and six caravans. Outside of major canoeing events like the Scottish Slalom Championships (www.canoeslalom.co.uk) and summer weekends, you may well find that you only have to share the campsite with a handful of other campers; when we stayed there were just two tents (including ours), a yurt and two small tourers. The campsite itself is located in an old railway station yard, which today is a pleasant green field surrounded by rolling hills and birch and oak trees. There is little here bar a facility block and two rope swings, which are slung from the enormous pine trees that dominate the camp.

With a dramatic natural setting strewn with birch and pine forests, dissected by the snaking River Tay and blessed with hills, lochs and mountains, it is no surprise that Perthshire is emerging as something of an adventure sports destination. Near Grandtully you can battle your way through rapids, fling yourself down flumes, plunge through waterfalls, chuck yourself off a cliff into water pools or clamber up a gorge; canyoning, cliff jumping and gorge walking can all be organised by local outfits. On Loch Tay itself you can take a ride on a novelty inflatable, a sailing course, a power boat course or a water-ski pull. Courses should be booked at least a couple of days in advance through the Adventure Perthshire Hotline (01577 861186; www.perthshire.co.uk) or directly with the operators listed on their website.

Freespirits (0845 6444755; www.freespirits-online.co.uk), are a company that pick up rafters outside the nearby River Inn and then whisk them up to Aberfeldy for an adrenaline fuelled ride (trips typically last 2–2½ hours). They say no group is too big or too small, taking booking for one person upwards at £30 per head. If the village slalom course and the roar of the river leave you yearning to take to the water in a kayak, a Canadian canoe or even an inflatable canoe there are other adventure operators based around in the Aberfeldy area.

As with the adventure trips, advance bookings need to be made for the campsite too, and the process is something of an adventure in itself. Text 07760 117641 for an entry code (we recommend checking the SCA website to make sure that this number is still current); this gives you access to the shower block. You also need to fill in a registration form (available inside the lobby of the campsite building or downloadable from the website), which you should then post, along with your camping fee in cash, in the security letterbox in the lobby.

As you set up your tent at your chosen pitch, your mind will quickly drift riverwards, stimulated by the sound of the gushing waters of the Tay and the rushing rapids, challenging you to test your skill and bravery.

THE UPSIDE: A green and usually quiet campsite with plenty of watersports on offer on the Tay.

THE DOWNSIDE: You can't actually see the River Tay from the campsite.

THE DAMAGE: Non-members £6 per person; SCA members £3 per person.

THE FACILITIES: Hot showers, toilets, dishwashing area, drinking water on tap, picnic benches and barbecues.

NEAREST DECENT PUB: Just 100 metres from the campsite the Riverside Inn (01887 840760) overlooks Grandtully's River Tay slalom course.

Even when canoes aren't flying past the window this is a good place for pub-style home cooking and Scottish ales.

IF IT RAINS: Take a trip back in time to Iron Age Scotland at the Scottish Crannog Centre (01887 830583) in Kenmore. A reconstructed loch dwelling and a chance to learn about an ancient way of life make it well worth the 12-mile trip.

GETTING THERE: Heading north on the A9 towards Inverness, look out for the right turn onto the A827 towards Ballinluig/Logierait. Follow the A827 until you reach Grandtully. Take the first left turn past the Riverside Inn and follow the road to the campsite.

PUBLIC TRANSPORT: You can catch the bus with Stagecoach Perth (01738 629339) from Perth Bus Station to Grandtully. The journey takes just over an hour. The same buses pick up in Aberfeldy, 25 minutes away.

OPEN: Mar–Oct.

IF IT'S FULL: Head to the *Cool Camping* site at Glengoulandie (p65).

SCA Grandtully Campsite, Grandtully, Near Aberfeldy, Perthshire	w	www.canoescotland.com
t	07760 117 641 (Send a text to request an entry code and check the website FAQs before ringing the number)	

ardgualich farm

Ardgualich Farm is one of those rough-around-the-edges anachronisms you cannot help but like. The local authorities have tried for decades to close down this simple site that predates the Second World War. Ardgualich has been in the same family since the war came to a close in 1945 and has somehow managed to rumble on into the 21st century still enjoying the epic scenery that first lured Queen Victoria to Loch Tummel back in the 19th century.

Queen Victoria fell in love with Loch Tummel to such an extent that she would scarcely let a trip to her beloved Scotland pass by without visiting at least once. Today, the spot where she perched and surveyed the slivery shadow of the loch as it drifted off from Perthshire towards the Highland peaks in the northwest is fittingly dubbed the 'Queen's View' and comes complete with a swish visitor centre. With numerous whisky distilleries nearby, world-class salmon and succulent local beef all wrapped around heather-clad hills and mountains, it is easy to see why a queen with a penchant for living the good life was drawn here.

Tales of world-famous monarchs seem a long way away at Ardgualich Farm, just down the road from the viewpoint. To say the site has no pretensions is as obvious as saying that Holland is a bit short on ski slopes. The old farm has been joined on its rumble down the grassy hillside towards the loch by a collage of caravans and some static homes, but there is still plenty of room for campers, who enjoy some of the best views from their grassy pitches. There is a family-orientated field near reception, but head right down the hill for the best spots. You can pitch your tent in the soft verges that fringe Loch Tummel, with only the sinewy sandy beaches and the lapping waves for company.

Whilst sitting by the water's edge is enough for some, others choose to get in, and not just those brave enough to risk a swim in the bracing loch. Campers are encouraged to bring their own small boats or canoes, though jet skis are mercifully banned. There is no launch charge at Ardgualich, leaving you free to explore the nooks and crannies of Loch Tummel at your own pace. Campers can also enjoy a free fishing permit and as you explore your primitive hunter-gatherer instincts and munch on freshly caught barbecued fish, the world of mobile phones and tortuous commutes seems very far away indeed.

Some of Loch Tummel's most famous inhabitants can be found above it rather than in it. Ospreys are now thriving around the shores of the loch after years of decline, when the very survival in Scotland of these impressive birds of prey was in doubt. Other flourishing residents you are likely to encounter are roe deer, who have been known to slip into the site and startle campers who wake to discover them nosing around their breakfast supplies.

Today Ardgualich Farm may not exactly have facilities and luxuries fit for a queen. What it does offer is a stripped-down camping experience with regal loch views, where you can get back to basics and barbeque your own fish as you idle your time away right by the edge of the loch. Queen Victoria's ghost, as it haunts the hills above, will no doubt be ever so slightly jealous.

THE UPSIDE: A queen's view for much less than a king's ransom.

THE DOWNSIDE: Caravans and statics dot the site but aren't too intrusive.

THE DAMAGE: £10 for a 2-person tent then 50p for each extra person.

THE FACILITIES: There is a basic toilet block and a hot shower.

NEAREST DECENT PUB: The Loch Tummel Inn (01882 634272) is an old-fashioned pub with a beer garden that overlooks the loch. Choose from the informal bar or loch-view restaurant. The homemade beef burgers and seared Shetland Salmon are both highly recommended. Good ales and whisky too.

IF IT RAINS: Pop into the Queen's View Visitor Centre to watch the short film about the area and then enjoy a pot of tea and a chinwag.

GETTING THERE: Heading north on the A9 from Perth towards Inverness take the B8019 exit towards Killiecrankie. Turn left for Tummel Bridge (you're still on the B8019) and follow the road for 6 miles, the entrance to the campsite is on the left.

PUBLIC TRANSPORT: The Pitlochry to Kinloch Rannoch bus operated by Broons Buses and Taxis (01882 632331) goes past the campsite.

OPEN: Mar–Oct.

IF IT'S FULL: Other nearby *Cool Camping* sites are located at Glengoulandie (p65) and Loch Tay (p61).

Ardgualich Farm & Loch Tummel Caravan Park, Ardgualich,

Pitlochry, Perthshire & Kinross PH16 5NS	t	01796 472825

red squirrel

Some people come to Scotland to delve deep into some of Europe's most spectacular mountains. Others come to explore the rich and brutal history, and still more to just enjoy a wee dram in the place where whisky began. If you fall into any of these categories, or ideally all three, the Red Squirrel is the place for you. It's a cosy campsite, dwarfed by a phalanx of towering Highland peaks in a glen draped in bloody history and home to one of Scotland's most famous pubs, where whisky drinking is practically obligatory.

The Red Squirrel lies in Glencoe, many Scots' favourite glen, which is praise indeed in a country that overflows with epic scenery. From the moment you begin the descent from the barren wastelands of Rannoch Moor, it's clear you're arriving somewhere special, as the road dips to acknowledge huge glacial massifs on either flank. If you're not an experienced walker, then this is foreboding stuff, as your eyes are drawn skywards, up scree-shattered slopes that appear infinite as they disappear into the high cloud. The visitor centre in the glen organises walks for those

not keen on heading out on their own; if you have the right gear and knowledge, check the weather forecast and you can just set off on one of the myriad hikes and climbs that break off all around.

The campsite is also perfect for those who enjoy mountains from a purely sedentary position. On a sunny day you can just laze around this grassy site, which spreads across 20 acres of meadow and woodland with a couple of burns snaking through it. The Red Squirrel describes itself as a 'casual farm site' and casual it is indeed with no official pitches. Push through to the end of the camp and follow the overgrown trail (you'll think you have gone the wrong way) and you can pitch on an isolated island with great views. Another plus is that the Red Squirrel allows fires, though not after 11pm when a silence rule descends on the camp.

The scene in Glencoe may be idyllic today, but it was one smeared with blood and terror in the hazy morning mist of February 13, 1692. Talk to any member of the MacDonald clan and it may as well have

been yesterday, for the pain they feel still simmers just below the surface. The government in London had long wanted to 'deal' with the troublesome MacDonalds and saw their chance when the clan did not sign a compulsory oath of allegiance to the king in time. They employed the Campbells of Glen Lyon who arrived to seek shelter and enjoy the hospitality of the MacDonalds (in time-honoured Celtic tradition). On the fateful morning they carried out their orders and massacred as many MacDonald men, women and children as they could lay their swords and daggers on; any bedraggled survivors were left to wander off into mountains through a descending blizzard.

After a hard day in the hills, or a traumatic one visiting the massacre memorial and the visitor centre that illuminates the glen's history, most campers seek refuge in the welcoming arms of the legendary Clachaig Inn. A sign at the door bans 'Hawkers and Campbells' and they are deadly serious – history in this part of the world is strictly of the living variety. All other visitors, though, are welcomed like long-lost cousins and soon you will be enveloped in a world of tall stories, live music and more than one or two wee drams.

THE UPSIDE: Epic mountain scenery laced with human drama.

THE DOWNSIDE: Toilets not the best especially during the busy summer season.

THE DAMAGE: £6.50 per person and children under 12, 50p.

THE FACILITIES: Simple toilet block with hot showers, water taps dotted around the site and a small information booth.

NEAREST DECENT PUB: The legendary Clachaig Inn (01855 811252) is staggering distance up the road back towards Glencoe. The Boots Bar is the place to be if you've just come off the hills covered head to foot in mud. The main lounge bar is a more comfortable spot with views out of the large windows; both serve hearty walker-friendly food with regular music.

IF IT RAINS: Learn about the nature and history of one of the most spectacular glens in Scotland at the eponymous Glencoe Visitor Centre (01855 811307). The home-baked cakes on sale in the coffee shop are divine.

GETTING THERE: Head north on the A82 from Stirling towards Fort William. About three-quarters of the way down Glencoe a right turn is signposted Clachaig Inn. Follow this single track down past the inn to the campsite.

PUBLIC TRANSPORT: Scottish Citylink (08705 505050) services from Glasgow stop at the Glencoe Visitor Centre.

OPEN: All year.

IF IT'S FULL: Camp at the small site by the official youth hostel a mile down the road towards the village of Glencoe.

| **Red Squirrel Campsite,** Glencoe, Argyll PH49 4HX | t | 01855 811256 | w | www.redsquirrelcampsite.com |

caolasnacon

Members of the *Cool Camping* team were here in June, pitched on the edge of the site, looking across the loch and out over the magnificent Mamore mountains. The weather was perfect, as it had been for days, but one particularly glorious evening we were sat outside, cooking over a small fire and we decided that camping life really couldn't get much better.

The site is situated down by the edge of the long seawater inlet of Loch Leven, where it narrows, halfway between the more open waters of Loch Linnhe and where the mountains bar the tides any further progress at the village of Kinlochleven. From the small promontory on which the lower half (and main camping area) of Caolasnacon lies, the view is made up entirely of a heady mix of mountains, trees, water and a bit of sky. The usual West Highland midge warning applies here, but the exposed loch-side pitches don't suffer as badly as those even a few yards inland. It's a very green and pleasant land in summer, but with some of Scotland's highest ground thrusting skywards from the arboreal pleasantries. Perfect.

A glorious scene, then, and one would assume life really couldn't get any better – but it did. As the fire died, the shadows lengthened and the sun started to slip away, a family of otters emerged from the seaweed and undergrowth on the margins of the loch and played happily in the shallows for more than an hour barely 10 metres from us. Whether it was familiarity with campers, our instinctive stillness or just good luck, we know not, but at one stage, those three otters got within three metres of our incredulous gaze.

The following day, with good weather still enveloping this scenic idyll, the sky was alive with buzzards soaring across the loch and the two resident golden eagles were patrolling the mountain slopes behind the site. No traffic could be seen or heard, and except for the other campers, of which there were few, no other trace of humanity trespassed into that wonderful moment in a wild place.

You could be forgiven for thinking that Caolasnacon is buried in the wastes hundreds of miles from anywhere else, but it

isn't; the main road from Glasgow to Fort William is just three miles away, at Glencoe.

Besides wildlife-watching, this site offers a chance to completely immerse yourself in one of the most beautiful places in Europe, and an opportunity to walk across some of Britain's most exciting mountains. The Mamores, directly across Loch Leven, are a wonderful walking place, whilst directly behind the site are the fearful rock walls of Glen Coe, where a steady head and two sure feet are a necessity. Canoeing in Loch Leven provides a different view of this scenic overload, and don't forget the bikes, as the pedal around Loch Leven is a truly great cycle route.

Within striking distance by car, on surprisingly good roads, are tourist centres such as Fort William and Oban, where distractions by boat (from Oban) and train (from Fort William) offer alternative or wet-weather entertainment. The Scottish Sealife Centre also provides an insight into what goes on deep in the loch that washes those beautiful shores just yards from your tent.

Caolasnacon is a unique opportunity to get away from it all, amongst some of the most appealing and least-spoilt scenery in the land but, amazingly, remains within easy reach of all those modern conveniences that make camping life enjoyable, whatever the weather has in store.

THE UPSIDE: Lovely loch-side location in classic highland scenery, and convenient for the main road south.

THE DOWNSIDE: None, besides the usual midge warning.

THE DAMAGE: From £8 for a 2-man tent and occupants, to £15 for a family.

THE FACILITIES: Not the most modern, but decent enough, and include free showers, toilets, washbasins, washing-up sinks, laundry, and electric hook-ups. Gas can be obtained at the farm.

NEAREST DECENT PUB: There is a good choice in Kinlochleven (3 miles) depending on what you're looking for: Chillers (01855 831100), in the Ice Factor, is quite trendy, with appropriate food; MacDonald's (01855 831539), not the American version, offers traditional hotel fayre; The Tail Race Inn (01855 831772) is a simple pub doing simple food, and Antlers Bar (01855 831202) is pie and a pint territory. The Seafood café, on the other side of the loch, offers an excellent selection of fresh and fulsome fish.

IF IT RAINS: The Ice Factor in nearby Kinlochleven has climbing walls, and the Scottish Sealife Centre near Loch Creran to the south is superb. Fort William is a 30-minute drive.

GETTING THERE: From the A82 (Glasgow–Fort William) road, take the B863 (right) in Glencoe, sign-posted Kinlochleven. The site is 3 miles on the left.

OPEN: Easter–Oct.

IF IT'S FULL: Good options nearby include Blackwater Hostel and Riverside Campsite (01855 831253; www.blackwaterhostel.co.uk) in Kinlochleven, The Red Squirrel Campsite (p79), or the Invercoe Caravan and Camping Park (01855 811210; www.invercoe.co.uk) situated in Glencoe village, with peaks all around.

Caolasnacon Caravan and Camping Park, Kinlochleven PH50 4RJ

| t | 01855 831279 | w | www.kinlochlevencaravans.com |

resipole farm

The Ardnamurchan peninsula on the western seaboard of the Highlands is the westernmost place in mainland Britain and despite being not that far north nor that far away from the hustle and bustle of Fort William, it is a surprisingly remote-feeling place. The quickest route here is by ferry, which enhances the isolated feel of the peninsula, but the difficulty in getting here helps preserve this beautiful area's peace and tranquillity.

To reach Resipole Farm, which lies next to the shining shores of Loch Sunart, involves a journey which is justification in itself for coming here; but be warned once here, not many want to drive home, despite the beauty of it all. Although this is a big campsite that gets quite busy mid-summer, the cumulative effects of big pitches, careful landscaping and the fact that everybody has a view of the loch and mountains results in a pleasant environment that doesn't feel hectic or busy. The facilities are excellent and well managed if these things matter, and they're still excellent, even if they don't.

What really matters here, though, is the world outside and all around Resipole Farm. If you spend your leisure time messing about in small boats – be it a canoe, sailing dinghy or small powerboat, the site is ideally placed and equipped to enable you to enjoy the vast expanse of Loch Sunart. The site's private slipway is just across the road and that's as far as you need to carry a canoe to be on the water.

Whilst the real essence of Ardnamurchan concerns the great outdoors, rather than civilised cultural matters, the Resipole Studios offer campers a unique opportunity to indulge their wallet on varying art forms, inspect the various exhibitions arranged in summer or even get involved themselves by attending tuition to improve their own artistic skills. Camping and culture in the same place? Whatever next...

If you take your bikes camping then this area is about as good as it gets for rampant cyclists, with the quiet loch-side road giving velocipedic access to rides as far as your legs will take you. And back of course. Castle Tioram is within easy biking reach, as are the lanes around the stunning sight of Kentra Bay, and the intimate wooded and muddy shores of Loch Moidart are best seen from the slow lane on a bike. Ardnamurchan Point is an ambitious pedal from Resipole (about 55 miles there and back) but the scenery viewed will ease the passage if not the pain, or you can just turn around when you've had half enough.

Walkers can enjoy themselves here, too, with a path leading out of the back of the site onto Ardnamurchan's very rough little mountains, and if the path is followed far enough, Ben Resipole will eventually (after about four miles) fall under foot.

One place that really must be seen whilst at Resipole is Sanna Bay, near Ardnamurchan Point. This vision of sand, sea, sky and hills is one of the most beautiful beaches on planet earth, and a visit here on the right day will linger very long in the memory. It's stunning. The road to Sanna Bay passes right through the centre of the very obvious remnants of a huge volcanic crater, and this is without doubt one of the most alien and exciting stretches of road in Britain. Awful to drive maybe (though nice to pedal), but geologically astounding.

Ardnamurchan is as gorgeous as it is unusual, and Resipole Farm offers civilised camping amongst this wonderfully exciting uncivilised place.

THE UPSIDE: Splendid location on the edge of Loch Sunart, in an unspoilt, largely undiscovered corner of Scotland.

THE DOWNSIDE: Despite the location, this is a big and sometimes busy site. (It can also be busy with midges.)

THE DAMAGE: Tent and two adults £11–13. Additional adults £3; children £1. Tent and two cyclists/backpackers £8.

THE FACILITIES: Modern and comprehensive amenities with showers, toilets, hot and cold to washbasins, dishwashing, laundry, disabled facilities, electric hook-ups and on-site shop selling the essentials.

NEAREST DECENT PUB: The Salen Inn (01967 431661) is two miles away, and fortunately it's a pleasant place where decent food can be found. About 5 miles away, Ardshealach Lodge (01967 431399) at Acharacle also has a good restaurant.

IF IT RAINS: Take either a stack of good books or your waterproofs (or both) or while away some time at the Resipole Studios.

GETTING THERE: From the A82 Glasgow–Fort William road, 10 miles south of Fort William, cross Loch Linnhe by the Corran Ferry then follow the A861 for about 20 miles to the site.

PUBLIC TRANSPORT: The bus from Fort William to Kilchoan, leaves at 1pm (Mon–Sat) arriving at Resipole at 2.30pm(ish).

OPEN: Apr–Oct.

IF IT'S FULL: Kilchoan Campsite (01972 510766), another 20 miles westwards, is a very different kind of site, being small with basic facilities, but has a glorious view and again is a cyclist's paradise.

Resipole Farm Caravan and Camping Park, Loch Sunart, Acharacle, Argyll PH36 4HX

| t | 01967 431235 | w | www.resipole.co.uk |

camusdarach

Camusdarach must surely be one of Britain's best all-round holiday destinations, but before getting into all the usual stuff, perhaps an explanation of the philosophy behind the running of the place may partially explain why a simple campsite can feel so thoroughly salubrious, and why everybody seems so relaxed and friendly whilst camping at Camusdarach.

The Simpsons (Andrew and Angela), from the Thames Valley, arrived in this little corner of coastal paradise some 12 years ago with a vision to turn a dilapidated farm and campsite into something special. But, because this is such a special place in the natural sense, they decided that everything would need to be eco-driven and completely sustainable. And they succeeded – it is extremely special.

Most of the day-to-day landscape management is done by a small flock of the endangered Hebridean sheep, whilst the trendy and very plush toilet block (renewable softwood) releases effluents into gravel beds and wetlands planted with specific plants whose job it is to detoxify the environment they grow in. There has

been no artificial landscaping of the two camping fields, because none is needed, and this whole philosophy of respecting nature and fitting in with it shines through to the everyday outlook of the running of the site. It's informal and friendly, and campers are treated as intelligent individuals, all of which is partly responsible for that indefinable feeling of wellbeing. In turn, everybody respects their neighbours and the site.

However, no matter how well run or eco-friendly a campsite may be, it is only really as good as the opportunities around it, and Camusdarach is engulfed by them. First and foremost are the seaside scenes that the site nestles amongst, with miles of dunes giving way to blindingly white sandy beaches. You can walk for miles along the strands here, never really coming to terms with the fact that this really is northwestern Scotland, and not the Caribbean. The islands of Skye, Rhum, Eigg, Canna and Muck punctuate the horizon across the azure waters, and you just can't help but feel good in this vision of paradise. Places like this sustain us through the long winters.

Many come here for a week and never move a motorised wheel for the whole duration, such is the basic appeal of the immediate surroundings, but another 'however' is due here, for the natural beauty of this area isn't restricted to this glorious seaside fringe. Visitors should turn their eyes inland to the lochs and hills for further inspiration, firstly towards Loch Morar, the deepest sheet of freshwater in Britain. Loch Morar is easy and rewarding to explore, be it on foot, partly by bike (from the site then on foot) or, better still, by canoe.

The road that leads to Camusdarach ends five miles further along at the small fishing port of Mallaig, which feels like a frontier town. It has the fascination of a real place (with shops if you need them), warts and all, and a place gripped by constant comings and goings. The big ferry to Skye is one such coming and going, whilst the supply ship to the Small Isles (Rhum, Muck, Eigg and Canna) makes a daily trip through amazing scenery.

From this superb little campsite, set in seaside heaven, you can stumble out everyday and gasp incredulously for weeks if the weather plays at all fair. And it often does here. There's nothing more to say and nothing more to write, as coming here is the only way to truly understand the feeling this place instils.

THE UPSIDE: Everything – the site, the location, the surroundings.

THE DOWNSIDE: Having to leave.

THE DAMAGE: £14 for tent and occupants on serviced pitch.

THE FACILITIES: Superb modern eco-block containing free showers, toilets, washbasins, disabled facilities, baby changing, dishwashing and laundry. Mobile shop visits twice weekly.

NEAREST DECENT PUB: The nearest is the Morar Hotel (01687 462346), which has a public bar equipped with a great selection of Malts, and the Silver Sands restaurant with a stunning view out over the beaches of Morar. Food is mainly traditional with salmon, trout, and venison on offer. The Cnoc-na-Faire Hotel (01687 450249) at Arisaig is highly recommended for its good food, whilst there is also a Thai takeaway (01687 462259) in Arisaig.

IF IT RAINS: Boat trips from Mallaig can be taken to the Isle of Skye on the ferry, or to Knoydart and Loch Nevis on the little boat that carries supplies and mail to the outlying farms with no road access. The train to Fort William from Mallaig is a memorable journey giving an armchair view of big scenery en route.

GETTING THERE: From the A830 Fort William–Mallaig road take the B8008 through Arisaig and along the coast. The site is on the left about 4 miles north of Arisaig.

OPEN: Mar–Oct.

IF IT'S FULL: Another *Cool Camping* site in the area is Invercaimbe (p101) 3 miles to the south of Camusdarach.

| **Camusdarach**, Arisaig, Inverness-shire PH39 4NT | t | 01687 450221 | w | www.camusdarach.com |

invercaimbe

There are numerous ways to describe a sunset: you can eulogise its fiery reds, deep oranges, the images of melting flames hitting the ocean, all the usual clichés and hyperbole. There is a sunset in Scotland, though, that may just manage to defy words. At Invercaimbe you can take a ringside seat on the beach by the campsite and take in the drama as the sun enjoys its dalliance with the Atlantic over the small isles of Rhum, Eigg and Muck in a setting bathed in a similarly deep glow of history.

This corner of the world possesses a real sense of the epic, the perfect backdrop for one of the most colourful periods in Scottish history, the '45' Jacobite rebellion whose mere mention still mists the eyes of many a Highlander. The unlikely and more than a little effete figure of Bonnie Prince Charlie landed at Glenfinnan in 1745 in an attempt to enlist the Highlanders in an audacious bid to reclaim his right to the British throne. After a shaky start and some understandable reluctance the clans massed and spent the ensuing months notching up victories as they built momentum on the charge south, reaching as far as Derby, spiralling London into a panic.

The failure of the rebellion – the Jacobites eventually retreated north and were brutally massacred on the moor of Culloden a year later – led to the complete break-up of Highland life as the British government banned the wearing of kilts, the playing of bagpipes and the clan system that had formed the backbone of Highland life for centuries. Its direct and indirect effects can still be felt in one of the EU's poorest regions today, adding a shade of pathos to the grandiose scenery as you stand on the beach that lies right in front of a campsite and enjoys a prime position on the sandy dunes overlooking the Atlantic.

The Invercaimbe Caravan and Campsite, which has only 20 pitches, lies right at the heart of Bonnie Prince Charlie country and makes a great base for exploring the legacy. You can visit Borrodale where the 'Young Pretender' first set foot on the mainland with only a handful of men rather than the promised 10,000 Frenchmen, and then head south to the visitor centre at Glenfinnan and see a re-creation of the day when the skirl of the pipes echoed around one of Scotland's most scenic glens for that last fateful massing of the clans, before returning to

Loch nan Uamh where he fled on a French frigate a year later, less than a mile from where his escapade began.

Once you have followed the history trail, Invercaimbe itself awaits with its simple pleasures. The wide sandy beach and sheltered sea inlet on two sides are perfect for paddling and swimming; they also hire out boats and ponies. This is the sort of place where you just tend to lose a day or two not doing very much, without even realising.

When the weather is glorious, there is no better place to be and when it is not, it just adds to the drama.

The highlight at Invercaimbe is, of course, one of those sharp breath-inducing sunsets. There is little point in trying to describe it; for a real picture you will fortunately need to come here for yourself. Suffice to say that Invercaimbe's sunsets provide a fitting background for departing princes and tragic lost causes.

THE UPSIDE: Epic drama from sunsets to Bonnie Princes.

THE DOWNSIDE: A lifetime wasted trying to find comparable sunsets afterwards.

THE DAMAGE: £8 for a 2-person tent.

THE FACILITIES: Toilets, showers, laundry, dishwashing room. There are 12 electric hook-ups.

NEAREST DECENT PUB: Whether you eat in the bar or the restaurant of the Arisaig Hotel (01687 450210) you will find a medley of fresh seafood.

The creamy East Coast Cullen Skink and the bouillabaisse made with fresh Highland fish and shellfish are both first class.

IF IT RAINS: Head south to the visitor centre at Glenfinnan (01397 722250) to follow in the Prince's footsteps. You can also join the world famous West Highland Railway from Arisaig down to Fort William, with a steam train on the route in summer.

GETTING THERE: Take the A830 from Fort William through Glenfinnan towards Mallaig. After

you pass through Arisaig look out for the signposts to Invercaimbe.

PUBLIC TRANSPORT: The Shiel Bus (01967 431272) service between Fort William and Mallaig passes the campsite on the A830.

OPEN: Easter–Oct.

IF IT'S FULL: Another *Cool Camping* site in the area is Camusdarach (p95) 3 miles north of here.

Invercaimbe Caravan and Campsite, Arisaig, Inverness-shire PH39 4NT

| | t | 01687 450375 | w | www.invercaimbecaravansite.co.uk |

faichemard farm

Imagine the scene. You arrive after a long journey at a gorgeous campsite and pitch in a secluded spot where the only sounds are the birds singing and the gentle breeze rustling through the trees. You skip off to the local pub and a few pints and a hearty dinner later, return full of the joys of camping. But then, the bucolic calm is shattered by the arrival of a frantic family of seven with a four-room mega-tent and a generator capable of powering a small town. The sounds of nature are replaced by incessant all-night kid-screaming and the thud of footballs bouncing off your tent. Mercifully, at Faichemard Farm this is an experience guaranteed not to happen, as this is one of the very few adults-only campsites in Scotland. The added bonus is a sweeping mountain backdrop and a location surrounded by forests.

At the end of Faichemard's first adults-only season (2006), owner Duncan Grant admitted that he had been overwhelmed by the response: 'We thought there might be a wee gap in the market, but nothing like this, with enquiries and campers pouring in from all over Scotland and from further afield too'. In addition to the ban on children, neither ball games nor cycling are allowed, though in no way is this a reflection of an unfriendly site, more indicative of a retreat for like-minded people looking for a quieter camping experience.

With only 40 pitches spread across an expansive 10-acre forest site, there is no danger of overcrowding and even in high season Grant is not tempted to squeeze in any more. The main, flat area is set around a small pond and is where most people congregate in summer when, on calm overcast days, the infamous Highland midge is out in force on the rest of the site. On sunny and breezy days, when midge activity is greatly reduced, the hillside pitches tempt with the chance to camp amongst the heather and enjoy your own private Highland retreat. Each pitch also has its own picnic table where you can munch away or enjoy a sundowner with the Glengarry mountains in the background.

With the adults-only policy and its enviable position amongst the hills and mountains, it is no surprise that Faichemard Farm is popular with walkers and climbers. Within easy striking distance is Ben Tee, whose 901-metre high mass can easily be seen from the campsite, as well as the more challenging mountains of Kintail.

The campsite also attracts walkers trekking the Great Glen Way, the most northerly of Scotland's two coast-to-coast walks, which cuts northeast from the railhead at Fort William in search of lochs Linnhe, Lochy, Oich and Ness, culminating at the Highland capital of Inverness.

Cycling may be banned at the site itself, but Faichemard Farm makes a good base for cycling on the Great Glen Way and for the world famous mountain biking tracks in the Nevis Range.

Whether you spend the day powering up to the dizzy heights of a Munro, cycling around Loch Ness or simply relaxing at the local pub, Faichemard Farm makes the perfect, quiet, kid-free retreat. The only unexpected noise may be the occasional sound of Duncan Grant coaxing a few tunes out of his trusty bagpipes, a sign that although this place is adult-only, it still manages to retain a sense of fun.

THE UPSIDE: An adult-only campsite that offers an oasis of calm.

THE DOWNSIDE: The midges are a problem amongst the trees and bushes; stick to the main campsite on overcast summer days.

THE DAMAGE: £8.50 per 2-person tent then £2 extra per adult.

THE FACILITIES: There are 2 toilet blocks with hot showers as well as shaver points, a tumble dryer and a washing machine.

NEAREST DECENT PUB: The Invergarry Hotel (01809 501206) may be a bit old-school, but it offers reasonable pub grub within walking distance. For a gastronomic experience head to the Old Pines (01397 712324), where the food more than rewards the drive.

IF IT RAINS: Learn more about the region's infrastructure at the Caledonian Canal Heritage Centre and the Clansmen Centre, which are both in nearby Fort Augustus.

GETTING THERE: From Inverness take the A82 along the north bank of Loch Ness. Turn right on to the A87 at Invergarry (signposted for Kyle of Lochalsh) and continue through the village for a mile. Turn right on to a minor road signposted Faichemard. Go past the other campsite (which may soon be turned into housing) and turn right at the 'A & D Grant, Faichemard Farm' sign.

PUBLIC TRANSPORT: Citylink buses (08705 505050) running between Inverness and Fort William stop at Invergarry.

OPEN: Apr–Oct.

IF IT'S FULL: Unfortunately, most of the sites around Loch Ness, to the north, are exclusively for caravans nowadays. Heading south, Linnhe Lochside Holidays (01397 772376; www.linnhe-lochside-holidays.co.uk) has a dedicated tent field amongst its lodges and statics, and a few waterside pitches.

Faichemard Farm Camping Site, Invergarry, Inverness-shire PH35 4HG

| | t | 01809 501314 | w | www.faichemard-caravancamping.co.uk |

shiel bridge

Shiel Bridge is a legendary place amongst mountaineers, and anybody with aspirations to stand astride the most handsome mountains in Scotland will eventually find themselves in Glen Shiel, staring up at the famous Five Sisters of Kintail or contemplating the steep and slightly perilous ascent of the mighty Forcan Ridge onto The Saddle. The campsite lies in the deep crevice of Glen Shiel, surrounded by these monsters, and it's fair to say that the view from your tent, in all directions, is of steep rock walls heading skywards.

It's a mesmerising place to just sit and stare, without even putting a single foot on the hills. It's a place for dedicated hill-folk certainly, but hills are only half the story here, because this is a startlingly good area for more generalised exploration.

Besides all those big, brave hills there are plenty of local, lower-level walks, notably the track up Glen Lichd (it goes on and on, with the only limit being your own), or the path over to Glen More on the Glenelg peninsula, and back via the Mam Rattagan Pass.

Still on an active theme, cyclists have ample opportunities to pedal through terrain varying from the near flat loch-side lane on the western side of Loch Duich to a marathon pedal over to Glenelg and back. Another tremendous on-road biking route is to take the bike around Loch Duich and Loch Long, then up Glen Elchaig to examine the Falls of Glomach, which after heavy rain are awesome. In truth, the off-road and on-road biking opportunities around Glen Shiel, Glenelg and Loch Duich are almost as endless as the walking routes.

If you're not a hillwalking superhero, what has Shiel Bridge got to offer more normal holidaymakers? Loads, is the answer. The Glenelg peninsula is one of the least-spoilt and least-trodden places in Scotland, stunningly beautiful and at Sandaig, you'll find the location where author Gavin Maxwell lived with his otters and wrote the definitive story of solitary life in the highlands, *Ring of Bright Water*. Then there are the wider attractions of Skye, with a distillery to examine, more waterfalls to gaze at, boat trips galore, and for general touring, the whole of Wester Ross to explore.

That very icon of Scottish scenes, Eilean Donan Castle, lies a few easy pedalling miles along the loch shore too, but expect to share it with every nationality under the sun, such is its celebrity status.

For a really great day by bike or car, go over the Mam Rattagan Pass, board the tiny car ferry to Skye then meander back through Skye to Kyle of Lochalsh, returning via the (now free) road bridge. A very different kind of journey can be taken on the railway from Kyle of Lochalsh to Inverness, as the train threads its way through one of Europe's most handsome and emptiest landscapes before arriving in the not-so-big city. If the weather was consistently kinder, all these attractions would make Shiel Bridge the Holy Grail of holidaying places.

The site itself is very civilised, with excellent shower and washing facilities, the provision of electric hook-ups and a decent food shop next door. As at all campsites on the west coast of Scotland, midge protection measures need to be thorough. So, whilst the atmosphere on the site reeks distinctly of all things mountaineery, it would be unfair to cast the place in such a singular role; Shiel Bridge is just as good as a scenic base-camp as it is home for hill-heroes. That said, just see if you can resist the lure of those hills.

THE UPSIDE: Totally immersed in magnificent scenery.

THE DOWNSIDE: Totally immersed in cloud and rain quite often.

THE DAMAGE: Tent and two adults £9.50; extra adults £4; children £2

THE FACILITIES: Modern and comprehensive, with toilets, showers, washbasins and electric hook-ups.

NEAREST DECENT PUB: The rather splendidly situated Kintail Lodge Hotel (01599 511275; www.kintaillodgehotel.co.uk) is a half-mile walk from the site, overlooking Loch Duich. It serves decent bar meals and also has a good restaurant.

IF IT RAINS: The iconic Eilean Donan Castle (01599 555202; www.eileandonancastle.com) is 6 miles away, or how about a trip on the Seaprobe Atlantis (glass bottomed boat) from Kyle of Lochalsh. (0800 980 4846; www.seaprobeatlantis.com).

GETTING THERE: Situated just off the A87(T) Kyle of Lochalsh road behind the shop at Shiel Bridge.

OPEN: Mar–Oct.

IF IT'S FULL: Other good sites in the area include the Caravan Club Site at Morvich (01599 511354) with level pitches surrounded by a stunning mountainscape, or Ardelve Campsite (01599 555231) for views of Eilean Donan Castle.

Shiel Bridge Campsite, Glenshiel, by Kyle of Lochalsh, Ross-shire, Highlands IV40 8HW   t   01599 511221

the shielings

The Isle of Mull, despite being one of the most southerly and easiest to access of the Inner Hebridean islands, is surprisingly unspoilt and very little molested by the tourist industry. Just about all the visitors to the island arrive on the impressive Caledonian MacBrayne ship, the MV *Isle of Mull*, which sails from Oban to the island's ferry terminal at Craignure. That such numbers travel to and from this sleepy little bay is quite bizarre. The two-hourly drama can be watched from the site as for a few minutes the place is thick with folk, then when the ship disappears, the place is deserted again, and you wonder whether it was all a dream.

The Shielings stands on the edge of the bay, overlooking the ferry terminal but also a colossal vista of glorious West Highland scenery taking in the Sound of Mull and Loch Linnhe, beyond which stand the highest hills in Britain. Besides having an extraordinary view, The Shielings is not just an ordinary campsite, as campers can have a choice of accommodation. Yes, you can bring your own tent and pitch it overlooking the scenery (or in a more sheltered position if you like), but you can chose from a variety of fixed 'shielings', which can be hired by the night or, more likely, the week. These shielings are, in effect, all-weather tents, and come equipped with beds, tables, chairs, a kitchen and even a heater. The posher models also have en-suite bathrooms. For those without the en-suite ablutional arrangements, the site facilities are excellent, so there's no excuse to rough it here.

Should you eventually tire of the view and the comings and goings at the ferry terminal, you can't help but notice, or indeed hear, the Isle of Mull Steam Railway chuntering back and forth across the seaward edge of the site. The station is just 100 metres away, and from there a narrow-gauge train takes passengers just over a mile to Torosay Castle and Gardens. In early summer, the garden is bright enough to hurt sensitive southern eyes, so remember to pack your shades. Another couple of scenic away-from-it-all miles on foot towards Duart Point reveals one of Scotland's classic sights, Duart Castle, which gradually grows nearer and more imposing. Back to Craignure, and if canoeing or sailing are your chosen sports, these can be launched at the front of the site into the Sound of Mull.

Even though Mull is an island, you can get to the mainland quickly and cheaply using the Fishnish–Lochaline ferry five miles north of the Shielings; it can seem easier to reach than other places that are actually on the mainland, such as Morvern or Ardnamurchan, which are incredibly remote.

Bring your bikes to Mull for some serious traffic-free miles, and a wilderness experience not found anywhere else in Britain. Another good bike ride is to the island's main (and only) town at Tobermory, at the northern end of Mull. It's a 40-mile round trip, but taken over the whole day, and in decent weather, it isn't nearly as arduous as it is scenic. Tobermory is famous for being the inspiration and setting for the kids TV show *Balamory*, but the island was famous before that for its wildlife, and especially its population of sea eagles. They can usually be seen around Loch Frisa, where there are organised eagle-spotting trips, but also at several other coastal areas on the island.

You don't need to be eagle-eyed to see the spectacular beauty of this island, and The Shielings is the perfect base from which to explore it all.

THE UPSIDE: Spectacular location, comfortable camping, easy access from ferry.

THE DOWNSIDE: Can get a little draughty.

THE DAMAGE: Tent and 2 people £14/14.50 low/high season, extra adults £4, children £2, dogs 50p; Shielings £26/169 per night/week for 2 adults; en-suite Shielings £39/254 per night/week; hostel £10 per night.

THE FACILITIES: Excellent amenities including free hot showers, toilets, washbasins, disabled facilities and laundry.

NEAREST DECENT PUB: The only pub in the area is The Craignure Inn (01680 812305) 200 yards away, and thankfully it's a good one with a varied menu. They also do takeaway pizzas. MacGregor's Roadhouse (01680 812471) is also handy, with top-notch grub.

IF IT RAINS: Torosay Castle and Gardens (01680 812421; www.torosay.com) are a 10-minute walk from the campsite, or get the ferry to Oban from the Craignure terminal, which is also less than 10-minutes away.

GETTING THERE: From the ferry terminal at Craignure turn left (south) and The Shielings is 300 metres on the left overlooking the bay.

OPEN: Easter–Oct.

IF IT'S FULL: Another *Cool Camping* site on the Isle of Mull is Fidden Farm (p125) at the extreme southwest of the island, or much nearer is Balmeanach Campsite (01680 300342) at Fishnish, 5 miles north. Facilities here are also excellent, and the site is more sheltered, but consequently the midges are more problematic.

| **Shieling Holidays**, Craignure, Isle of Mull PA65 6AY | t | 01680 812496 | w | www.shielingholidays.co.uk |

fidden farm

Fidden Farm isn't so much a campsite as a place to camp, and if there's nobody camping, which is quite common in the marginal months, then it is impossible to distinguish the place from any other stretch of deserted unspoilt coastline where the odd sheep is whiling away the day enjoying the view. There are no signs telling you that you've arrived at a campsite (well no signs telling you anything actually) and many a baffled camper must surely have turned around, disappointed, and left thinking that maybe there isn't a campsite here after all. But there is, and it's thriving in a very quiet way.

The drive to Fidden Farm from the ferry terminal at Craignure is just short of 40 miles, and besides being one of the loveliest 40 miles on the planet they are probably also some of the longest – as the road bucks and bobs its single track way through, round, over and under a variety of scenery as diverse as any in Britain. It's worth a couple of nights camping at Fidden Farm just for the experience of the journey to get there, and back. Especially if your chosen means of motivation is a bike.

When scenery-stained campers eventually arrive at Fidden Farm, still reeling from the sights en route, what they stumble upon is almost as unexpected as it is enchanting. The site (but not a site) stands on several acres of close-cropped wind-blown turf that meanders along the coast in a series of small bays, enclosed by low, granite headlands with crystal clear turquoise waters lapping over dazzling white sand beaches. Once here, you'll find it is completely impossible not to stand and stare; managing to do anything that requires you to be inside your tent will be short of miraculous.

All in all, it takes a good couple of days to calm down, let the mental metabolism adjust to 'Fidden Farm time' and come to terms with your good fortune in finding the place. Bring everything you have in the way of bikes and canoes, and be prepared to use them; the heavily indented coastline of Mull makes it perfect for sea kayaking, and the traffic-free roads are as biker friendly as they are joyously scenic.

Most of the time Fidden Farm is getting-away-from-it-all-camping in no uncertain

terms, but apparently, for the first two weeks of the English school holidays, half the nation feels the urge to escape and a good proportion, it seems, migrate here, so choose your time wisely.

So, what else is there to do besides canoeing, biking, bird-watching or just wandering about in a trance of slightly detached amazement? Surely that's enough? If not, the pilgrimage to the island of Iona can be made from Fionnphort either for purely sightseeing reasons or for a lovely stroll around the entire island (about 9 miles). Those with deeper religious intent may want to visit Iona Abbey, where Christianity was first washed up on these beautiful shores. And whilst prowling around Fionnphort, waiting for a ferry, the café and shop can be inspected too. The shop stocks everything you're likely to need, including the famously delicious Selkirk Bannock Bun, a rich fruit bun that is all anybody really needs in life. Also accessible from Fionnphort is the small uninhabited island of Staffa, which resembles the Giant's Causeway in Northern Ireland. And that's it – anything else is miles (and miles) away, but that's the whole point of getting away from it all.

THE UPSIDE: Far, far from the madding crowd, and in an incredibly beautiful location.

THE DOWNSIDE: Life can get a bit breezy here.

THE DAMAGE: £4 per adult per night, £2 per child.

THE FACILITIES: A well-maintained portakabin at the farm contains free showers, toilets and a small washbasin in each gender-specific half and there's an external washing-up sink. It is quite a trek from the camping field and the only tap is also next to the farm.

NEAREST DECENT PUB: There is only one, and thankfully the Kell-Row is a good one, only just over a mile from the site, and offers excellent traditional food and beers.

IF IT RAINS: Take a few good books, or be prepared to get wet canoeing, walking or cycling.

GETTING THERE: Take the A849 from the ferry terminal at Craignure signposted to Fionnphort and Iona, then in the centre of Fionnphort, turn left into the lane to Fidden Farm.

OPEN: Easter–Oct.

IF IT'S FULL: There is another *Cool Camping* site on the Isle of Mull at The Shielings (p119), though this is of a very different nature. If getting-away-from-it-all is the order of the day then consider the 'official' wild camping place at Calgary Bay (p216) on the northwestern shore of the island.

Fidden Farm Campsite, Knockvologan Road, Near Fionnphort, Isle of Mull PA66 6BN t 01681 700427

glenbrittle

When was the last time you saw the Milky Way? Or had no signal on your mobile? In this remote glen on the Isle of Skye, far away from the ubiquitous glow of sodium street lamps and the tinny clamour of downloaded ringtones, a hazy white ribbon stretches across the clear and silent night sky. If you watch for long enough you're bound to see the streak of a shooting star and if you listen carefully enough you'll hear nothing at all. It's an ideal opportunity to reacquaint yourself with constellations you know only from newspaper horoscopes and with the pleasures of total silence.

Glenbrittle is not one of those sites with shiny toilet blocks, tumble dryers and chiller cabinets full of fizzy drinks for the kids. This vast tract of Skye is owned by the Macleod clan who gained public prominence a few years ago by trying to sell the Cuillin mountains for the bargain price of £10 million. Curiously, buyers were thin on the ground. Rumours abound of an upgrade of the facilities at Glenbrittle but for the time being, the site's rugged simplicity is part of its attraction. It is a little like a links golf course, with smooth broad fairways in which to pitch your tent and knee-deep rough in which to lose stray tent pegs.

If you do misplace any, the campsite's shop, run by the gregarious Alex MacGregor, will sell you some replacements. Alex is one of those annoyingly sunny people who are the envy of city dwellers. He spends half the year amid the beauty of Glenbrittle and the other half travelling in Asia. His worldly ways are useful in a site that attracts an eclectic clientele from all corners of the world. You may stumble upon Scottish hippies singing Ziggy Stardust around a fire on the beach, cooking up the mussels they've collected from the shore, a gaggle of Polish climbers returning to the site from the Cuillin hills, jangling their crampons and carabiners or a quiet Japanese couple with a state-of-the-art tent and a worrying collection of sashimi knifes. Just don't let them see the Pot Noodle you're cooking up for supper.

Those of a healthy disposition should visit the Fairy Pools, a few miles back up the single-track road that leads to Glenbrittle. This series of mountain pools and streams sits in the lee of the mountains and, though

the water is freezing even in summer, a breathless dip here has more restorative power than the swankiest health spa. Or if you have been climbing the mountains above, the pools provide the perfect opportunity to cool down before heading back to camp.

Glenbrittle is probably most popular with climbers, who use it as a base for tackling the Cuillins, the mountain range that dominates the Skye skyline. Like a jaw full of broken and blackened teeth, it looms over Glenbrittle, blotting out the early sun. Every morning, plucky climbers can be seen setting off up the hill at dawn but quickly look as small as hobbits against the mountains. Climbing here is a serious business and not for the faint-hearted. But even if you are not part of the carabiner and crampon crew, Glenbrittle is the perfect tonic for anyone who wants peace, tranquillity and a mobile phone with no signal.

THE UPSIDE: Great views of the Milky Way and free mussels on the beach.

THE DOWNSIDE: The showers, though hot, rely more on gravity than water pressure to get you wet.

THE DAMAGE: £4.50 per adult and £3.50 per child (5–15 years); under-5s go free.

THE FACILITIES: Rather rustic wash block. Hot showers and drinking water available and an outdoor dishwashing area with a single cold tap. There is a campsite shop for basic provisions.

NEAREST DECENT PUB: The Old Inn (01478 640205) at Carbost 8 miles back up the single-track access road, has regular live music and a lively atmosphere. For those who prefer fine ales or single malts, try the bar at the Sligachan Hotel (01478 650204).

IF IT RAINS: Visit the Talisker Distillery at Carbost (01478 614308). Talisker is one of the smokiest, peatiest malts around.

GETTING THERE: From the Skye Bridge follow the A87 to Sligachan. Turn left onto the A863 at the sign for Dunvegan. After 5 miles, turn left for Carbost on the B8009 and follow the road for 2 miles until the sign for Glenbrittle and the single track road down to the sea.

OPEN: Apr–Sep.

IF IT'S FULL: There is a 36-bed youth hostel (0870 004 1121) a few miles back up the road and the Waterside Bunkhouse at the Old Inn in Carbost (01478 640205).

Glenbrittle Campsite, Carbost, Isle of Skye IV47 8TA

| | t | 01478 640404 | w | www.dunvegancastle.com |

sligachan

The western fringe of Scotland is a place completely set apart from the rest of Britain by its remarkable mixture of big rocky mountains, beautiful lush green valleys and seductive sandy shorelines. Nowhere else soothes the troubled urban soul quite like this northern paradise.

Well, that's the western fringe of Scotland for you, summed up in a sentence or two, but not the Isle of Skye. For this remarkable island is as different from the west of Scotland as the northwestern fringe is from the southeast of England. Skye doesn't do soothing, or soft, and Skye certainly doesn't do a lot of green. Skye is elemental, savage, bare, boggy and yet a hard mistress. But like all forms of basic beauty Skye is completely addictive and once seen (in the right light) eats into your soul and never loses its grip. You spend your southern days waiting for the next trip north, and right in the middle of all this fanciful soul-searching savagery sits Sligachan campsite – a victim and a victory all in one place.

Dealing with sensible, practical matters first, the site's ablutional facilities are acceptable and more than adequate, if not plush. The squat stone building containing them reflects the harshness of the world outside, and this has somehow crept inside too. If bad weather persists it also seems to seep inside the mind, but thankfully the weather around here can best be described as 'fast'. And 'fast' weather is good, for it slows down the whole world's supply of midges leaping out of the boggy wastes surrounding the site, brandishing their teeth.

There are good grounds for suggesting that Britain should set up its Olympic Training Village at Sligachan, as several world records are broken on any given evening when the midges are about. It's about 400 metres from the centre of the site to the pub door, and from tent to bar, wearing big boots and anorak, it takes the average camper 19.8 seconds to cover the distance with a million midges in pursuit. Astounding.

If you're getting the impression that we're attempting to put you off a visit to Sligachan then there may be some truth in that assumption, but we do believe in painting a true picture of things. It is, of course, almost incidental that we might want the place to ourselves, for when things turn out right here, when the sun shines

(and the midges can't stand the heat), then we who have been victims want to enjoy the spoils exclusively. And when things are right, some of the roughest, rockiest, most savage scenes on the island sit directly behind the hotel and campsite, daring you to dip even a toe into their territory.

Even getting to Sligachan from the Skye Bridge is an experience always remembered, as the road winds through the big hills of the Red Cuillins into the very centre of the island, where the campsite and the fearful-looking Black Cuillins await your flimsy nylon. But the most outrageous thing about Skye is that the most outrageous scenes of all, up on the Trotternish peninsula, and all around the pinnacled northern coast haven't even been glimpsed as yet.

No, Skye isn't comfortable, but it's a place worth persevering the pain to discover, and Sligachan is the place to gainfully employ yourselves in that process.

THE UPSIDE: Slap bang in the centre of the craziest scenery in the realm.

THE DOWNSIDE: Slap bang in the centre of the craziest midge-breeding scenery in the realm.

THE DAMAGE: £4 per adult, children 5–13 years £2 and under-5s free.

THE FACILITIES: A bit rough and ready for some, but it is reasonably equipped with showers, toilets, washbasins, electric hook-ups and basic laundering facilities.

NEAREST DECENT PUB: One of the great pubs of the world, The Sligachan Hotel (01478 650204), is directly across the road. They serve enormous meals, a baffling variety of ales and every variety of Scotch known to (Scots) man. The atmosphere is terrific too.

IF IT RAINS: See 'Nearest decent pub'.

GETTING THERE: The site is next to the main road running up through Skye (A850) from the bridge to Portree.

OPEN: Easter–Oct.

IF IT'S FULL: Glenbrittle campsite (p131) lies across the other side of this colossal pile of scenery.

Sligachan Campsite, Sligachan, Isle of Skye IV47 8SW | t | 07786 435294 | w | www.sligachan.co.uk

cnip village grazing trust

If you've never felt like you've reached the end of the earth then come to Traigh na Beirigh (don't try to pronounce it) near Cnip (pronounced 'neep'). This tiny crofting community on the western coast of Lewis in the Outer Hebrides seems like the last place on earth. In reality, if you kept going west you'd eventually end up on the Labrador coast of Newfoundland (where there's probably someone looking east feeling the same as you) but you'd never guess it standing on the dunes of Traigh na Beirigh gazing out over the aqua blue water. It feels like the end of everywhere you've ever been. And that, of course, is the attraction. Even the cluster of cottages that comprise Cnip is over the hill in the neighbouring bay so the only thing to disturb the peace is that occasional bang of a grousing gun in the hills behind and the sound of the waves on the beach.

Traigh na Beirigh is the name of the bay on whose grassy dunes the campsite sits. The site is owned by the Cnip villagers through a community trust and is administered by Agnes Maclennan, a charming woman who lives at Number 15. Visitors are ushered into her home whilst she writes out a receipt for the camping fees. She keeps a warm kitchen, even in the summer, where the heat of the old Aga and Agnes' lilting west-coast accent, a mix of Scots and Irish, could lull an insomniac to sleep.

Cnip is 40 miles from Lewis's only real town, Stornoway, over miles and miles of captivating emptiness in which rocks poke through the threadbare soil like elbows through an old tweed jacket. Agnes's burning Aga is a sign that even in the summer, the weather on Lewis can be cold and harsh, and the landscape elemental and bleak. And so the bay, when it comes, is something of a surprise. The road from Cnip climbs the shoulder of the hill and as you crest the brow the aqua blue bay is suddenly there before you with its scimitar of white sand fringed with grass.

Compared with some of Scotland's other bays, though, Traigh na Beirigh is modest. If you really want to stretch your legs, then head for Uig Sands, four miles south of Cnip. It's an extravagant bay where the low tide retreats for miles out to sea and leaves

a rippled tract of golden sand over which to range. It was here that a cow accidentally found the Lewis Chessmen in 1831. Made by the Vikings from walrus ivory, these 12th-century chess pieces were discovered amongst the sands and are now in the National Museum in Edinburgh.

Old though the ancient chessmen are, even they are new kids on the block in comparison with Lewis' main attraction, the Standing Stones at Callanais. These swirling spires of Lewisian Gneiss, the oldest rock in Britain, have the gnarled look of petrified oak trunks. As well they might because the stones, set in the shape of a Celtic cross, are older than Stonehenge and just as baffling.

The runic allure of the stones attracts its fair share of hiking hippies, the rocky equivalent of tree huggers, who come to commune with the stones, much to the frustration of photographers in search of that cherished shot (and much to the amusement of the incurious sheep). Neither can ruin the simple grandeur of Callanais, though, particularly as dusk begins to fall. If you can get a shot of the stones at sunset, it will definitely be one to keep.

And back at Cnip, sunrise over the waters of the bay is another finger clicking moment to cherish long after you've gone home to tell your friends of your stay at the end of the earth.

THE UPSIDE: Stunning setting at the end of the world.

THE DOWNSIDE: The empty caravans of the Stornoway Caravan Club are parked at the site over the summer.

THE DAMAGE: Small (2-person) tent £4; large tent £5.

THE FACILITIES: One small but serviceable toilet block with male and female facilities (one cubicle and two coin-operated showers each) and a dishwashing station. There is a recycling facility behind the toilet block.

NEAREST DECENT PUB: There are more churches than there are pubs on Lewis. The Uig Community Shop 4 miles south of Cnip at Timsgearraidh is licensed and sells a modest range of beers, wines and spirits.

IF IT RAINS: Think up new similes for the sound of rain on your tent. Like popcorn popping in a pan, for example.

GETTING THERE: From Stornoway follow the A859 to Leurbost and turn right to Achmor. Then take the B1011 to Miabhig. Take a right and follow the road through Cliobh to Cnip. Stop at

Number 15 at the bottom of the hill and pay.

PUBLIC TRANSPORT: There is a bus service (Number W4) from Stornoway to Uig with a separate service for the loop road through Cnip.

OPEN: Apr–Oct.

IF IT'S FULL: There is an informal camping area about 5 miles south at Uig Sands. It costs £1 per person, there is a small portakabin toilet with standpipe about quarter of a mile away but that's it. Pay at 6 Ardroil before following the dirt track to the sands.

| **Cnip Village Grazing Trust Campsite**, Cnip, Uig, Isle of Lewis HS2 9HS | t | 01851 672265 |

lazy duck

It says everything about the Lazy Duck that their half dozen Aylesbury ducks are too lazy to even bother hatching their own eggs. Not for them, toiling to keep their eggs warm and then the hassle of having to rear their young. Oh no, they are far too busy relaxing around the lush pond, sunning themselves amongst the heather or seeking shade under the protective shelter of the giant Scots pines that rise all around.

The Lazy Duck seems to have a similarly soporific effect on campers too. It may be less than a mile from the nearest village at Nethybridge, but the rough single-track road takes you into another world, one where the towering massif of the Cairngorms dominates the background and the foreground opens up with gently twittering birds, swaying hammocks and rope swings.

The campsite was added in 2002 to a location that is still best known for the excellent Lazy Duck Hostel, which has been much eulogised in various guidebooks and is legendary amongst walkers and the odd (make that really quite odd) honeymooning couple. The campsite is very small indeed and booking is essential, with space for only four pitches, though the charming couple behind the Lazy Duck, David and Valery Dean, have been known to help out walkers in an emergency. The tents nestle in a small glade surrounded by trees. There is a rope swing, a hammock where you can idle away a few hours and a picnic bench complete with a chiminea to keep you warm on chillier evenings. The 'bush shower' is a defiant stand against the British climate, an outdoor solar-heated experience introduced by the Dean's son who got the idea while working in Africa.

The two most popular spots at the Lazy Duck are the 'heather hammock' and the sauna. The former is a simple hammock stretched out between two trees in an idyllic spot away from the hostel and campsite. The views are sublime, with the heather moorland and patches of Caledonian forest stretching out in front, while the peaks of the Cairngorms, now protected as a national park, lurk to the rear. The sauna is not just an afterthought either, with a small chill-out area by the sauna room where you can light a candle, burn a little essential oil and listen to their collection of ambient CDs.

If you manage to rouse yourself from this wanton relaxation – no mean task here – then even setting out on a walk requires little effort, as the Speyside Way, one of Scotland's designated network of marked long-distance trails, passes nearby. The area is also very popular with mountain bikers and you can cycle on the Speyside Way itself, around the Abernethy Forest or the Rothiemurchus Estate. The forest and estate are both highly regarded with a variety of terrains, from smooth forest roads to tough muddy single tracks through the thick trees. In winter there are ski fields nearby; the Deans advise people to bring their own sleigh if they fancy a spot of sledging.

Back in the campsite, one of the simple pleasures is just watching the eponymous ducks amble through their day. They are joined in the ponds and Fhuarain burn by myriad other birdlife including mandarin, wigeon, pintail, whistling duck and capercaillie. They may not exactly qualify as ideal parents, but the Lazy Ducks may have a thing or two to teach stressed-out visiting campers with their relaxed approach to life.

THE UPSIDE: The perfect place to get lazy.

THE DOWNSIDE: Not many pitches and a maximum 4-night stay; you will want to stay longer.

THE DAMAGE: £7 for a tent with one person, £3 per extra person.

THE FACILITIES: Hot and cold water, washing-up space, 'bush shower', sauna, wet-weather cooking shelter and free-range eggs (when available).

NEAREST DECENT PUB: The slick, comfortable Nethybridge Hotel (01479 821203) is within easy walking distance of the campsite. Enjoy a dram or a pint in the lounge bar or have a hearty meal in the Abernethy Restaurant.

IF IT RAINS: The MacDonald Highland Resort (0845 608 3734; www.aviemorehighlandresort.com) in Aviemore is a great wet-weather base as you can stay there and use their swimming pool, eateries and also organise a variety of sports and day trips from here.

GETTING THERE: From Aviemore take the A95 east and turn off to the unclassified road to the right signposted for Nethybridge. Then turn left on to the B970, and right on to another unclassified road to enter Nethybridge. The campsite is on the edge of the village right off the Tomintoul road.

PUBLIC TRANSPORT: Highland Country Buses (01479 811211) run services to Nethybridge from Aviemore and Grantown-on-Spey.

OPEN: All year.

IF IT'S FULL: Wild camping in the heather, with the usual wild camping sensibilities (p215). You can also stay at the Lazy Duck Hostel on-site, one of Scotland's best.

Lazy Duck Campsite, Nethybridge, Inverness-shire PH25 3ED

| | t | 01479 821642 | w | www.lazyduck.co.uk |

rothiemurchus

If you like trees – seriously like trees – then Rothiemurchus campsite is the type of spot you might go to and never want to come back from. It's one of the best places in Scotland to enjoy swathes of indigenous Caledonian woodland, with a flurry of Scots pine, birch and juniper forest and wood-shrouded lochs. There is a real sense of being somewhere genuinely unspoilt and pristine here: clear evidence of how the land was formed during the last Ice Age 10,000 years ago and timeworn trees that will make you feel seriously mortal.

The award-winning campsite is set within the boundaries of the Rothiemurchus Estate, which itself lies right on the edge of the remarkable Cairngorm Mountain massif, the vast mountain plateau that was recently designated the UK's largest national park. There are caravans and static homes on the site, but trees quickly conceal these to leave you adrift in your own Forest of Eden. You can choose from the main pitches, where you will see other tents and be close to the amenities, or you can head across one of the burns that rumble through the camp, the largest of which is the Am Beanaidh. It is a sublime experience waking up on a bed of

soft needles on a summer morning to the sound of rushing water with the smell of pine spiking the crisp air.

Man has been attracted to this woodland area since at least the Bronze Age. By the late 1500s, the land had fallen under the control of John Grant of Freuchie who bestowed it upon his second son, Patrick, the first Grant laird of Rothiemurchus. The Grant family has held the stewardship of the Estate for over 400 years to the present day and have proved enlightened landowners, opening up the land for walkers and cyclists, as well as tree lovers. Scotland's lingering feudal land ownership attracts its share of controversy, but Rothiemurchus is the type of inclusive estate that the Land Reform Act was designed to encourage.

You can hire bikes from the visitor centre on the estate and meander around the myriad paths, with an easy circular route taking in the twin lochs of Morlich and Loch an Eilein. The latter is one of the prettiest in the country with a ruined castle sitting in the middle of the water and beaches fringing its edges. There are some more serious routes up past the outdoor activity

centre at Glenmore that stretch up into the mountains on old drover's trails opening up remote lochs and isolated bothies.

Glenmore Lodge (01479 861256; www.glenmorelodge.org.uk) is a serious outdoor activity centre with a particular emphasis on climbing and mountaineering, being handy for the Cairngorms and some of Britain's finest ice climbing, as well as plenty of summer routes. Novices can either seek their advice or enrol on one of their frequent courses. If that's all a bit too adventurous, just climb aboard the Cairngorm Mountain Railway, the funky funicular railway that eases up the mountainside revealing stupendous views with minimal effort. Be aware, though, that walkers cannot use the funicular and equally that funicular users cannot push on to the summit.

Rothiemurchus is the sort of site that ticks so many different boxes. It works for those looking to get away from it all, those wanting to fling themselves around on a bike or those who fancy a walk off into the challenging Cairngorm Mountains. And with all those trees around, it really grows on you.

THE UPSIDE: Trees, trees and yet more trees. Think of all those wonderful endorphins they will pump through your system.
THE DOWNSIDE: The caravan site as you come in is a bit off-putting; some reports suggest the staff can be a touch unfriendly but were fine on our visit.
THE DAMAGE: £5 per person.
THE FACILITIES: Keycard operated shower block with hot showers and toilets.

NEAREST DECENT PUB: The Old Bridge Inn (01479 811181) is only 2 miles away on the road to Aviemore. This atmospheric old inn now specialises in great seafood and local lamb, with plenty of whiskies and real ales on hand.
IF IT RAINS: Rothiemurchus Estate lies just outside the resort town of Aviemore, the self-styled 'Adventure Capital of the Highlands', with its numerous amenities. The Macdonald Highland Resort is a fully equipped resort with swimming pools and restaurants (www.aviemorehighlandresort.com).

GETTING THERE: Rothiemurchus Campsite is just a couple of miles off the A9. Coming north take the first turning for Aviemore and then follow the signs for Rothiemurchus. The site is visible after a couple of miles on the right hand side.
PUBLIC TRANSPORT: Highland Country Buses (01479 811211) run services from Aviemore to the Cairngorm Mountain Railway, passing the campsite on the way.
OPEN: All year.
IF IT'S FULL: Head for the *Cool Camping* site at the Lazy Duck (p149).

Rothiemurchus Camp and Caravan Park, Rothiemurchus Estate, By Aviemore, Inverness-shire PH22 1QH

| | t | 01479 812800 | w | www.rothiemurchus.net/caravanpark.html |

torridon

If the thought of spending the night without a hot shower or flushing toilet makes your blood curdle but you fancy the freedom of wild camping, then you're in a bit of a quandary. The solution is on hand, though, in the form of the Torridon Campsite. Open only to tents and often deserted, this gem is as close to wild camping as you can get, but with toilets and hot showers on hand to ease you through the experience.

Despite being located just off the A896 at the entrance to Torridon village and opposite the Torridon Countryside Centre, this small field still manages to feel both incredibly remote and rustic. Rowan trees and Scots pine shield the campsite from the road, and the basic toilet and shower block is actually located just outside the main gate – although they belong to the campsite they are also open to the public. The fact that you are allowed to build campfires, as long as you contain them, use twigs and branches that are lying on the ground and don't cut any wood from the trees, is also a big plus. The campsite's crowning glory, though, is the voluminous Liathach massif that looms large from above the northern perimeter; although Torridon's volatile weather and frequent low cloud cover mean that you might only see the boulder fields on the mountain's lower slopes.

In keeping with wild camping, you cannot book a pitch in advance and there is no charge to stay at Torridon. In fact, the only drawback you might face is that it can get boggy if it's been raining, so pitch on the perimeter and park in the Countryside Centre car park. Also, in overcast weather with little wind, the midges can be ferocious, so don't forget to bring your Avon Skin So Soft.

Torridon, a mesmerising, protected landscape of sweeping sea lochs, tumbling burns and hulking mountain peaks that vault towards the heavens, is one of Scotland's last great wildernesses and a Mecca for walkers and climbers. Together, the Achnashellach and Torridon hills boast no less than 17 Munros (peaks over 900 metres high). The views from the top of Torridon's peaks are breathtaking; however, these are serious mountains, where wild weather, knife-edge ridges and vertical ascents make them hazardous for even the most experienced climber, so caution must be exercised.

Single track road

Use passing places to permit overtaking

It is advisable to tackle more difficult walks in the company of a guide. Low- and high-level walks can be booked with rangers from the Countryside Centre (01445 791221; Easter–Sep). You can also book a host of activities with Torridon Activities (01445 791242; www.torridon-activities.com), including an excellent navigation course that equips you with the skills to find your way back off the mountains in reduced visibility.

An alternative is to follow one of the area's classic lower-level trails to Coire Mhic Fhearchair. It takes around two hours to reach the coire from the A896 car park, but the ascent doesn't really get steep until you reach the waterfalls that signal your imminent arrival. The centrepiece of this stunning coire is the eponymous Loch Mhic Fhearchair, whose crystal-clear waters reflect the ancient sandstone hulk of the triple buttress that flanks its southern edge.

At the end of a strenuous day's walking amidst some of Scotland's most impressive mountain scenery, you can, as you wash away any aches and pains in a free hot shower and settle down to a meal cooked on your campfire, celebrate your decision not to wild camp. If you can bear to take another short walk or an easy drive, dusk brings hordes of wild stags down to the roadside just to the north. The perfect end to your almost wild camping day.

THE UPSIDE: You often have the deer and mountains all to yourself.

THE DOWNSIDE: The ground can be boggy if there has been a lot of rain.

THE DAMAGE: There is no charge and bookings are not taken.

THE FACILITIES: Toilets, hot showers and sinks with hot and cold water. The toilet block is located just outside the campsite and can be used by the general public.

NEAREST DECENT PUB: Three miles from the campsite (on the A896 towards Shieldaig) the Ben Damph Inn (01445 791242) is a welcoming bar and restaurant. A menu that keeps walkers firmly in mind features hearty pub grub including haddock and chips, steak and burgers, and wickedly calorific desserts.

IF IT RAINS: Put on your waterproofs and prepare to brave the elements, but stick to low-level walks. Or chill out at the Ben Damph Inn (see above), which also has rooms.

GETTING THERE: Heading north on the A9 from Inverness take the A835 towards Ullapool then the A832 towards Gairloch. After Kinlochewe turn left onto the A896 (signposted Shieldaig) and look out for the right turn to Torridon. The campsite is on the right.

PUBLIC TRANSPORT: Duncan MacLennan Buses (01520 755239) operate services from Strathcarron to Torridon via Shieldaig, and from Lochcarron via Kishorn. Royal Mail Post Bus services (08457 740740) run to Torridon from Achnasheen via Kinlochewe.

IF IT'S FULL: The Torridon Youth Hostel (0870 0041154) charges £12 for a dormitory bed. You can also camp on common grazing land in Shieldaig, although the site doesn't have any facilities.

Torridon Campsite, Torridon, Achnasheen, Ross-shire

t | Info from Torridon Countryside Centre (01445 791221; Easter–Sep, 10am–5pm) or Highland Council (01349 868479)

the wee camp site

As names go, they don't come any more appropriate. The Wee Camp Site does exactly what it says on the tin, offering a stripped-down camping experience on one of the smallest sites in Scotland. The brother and sister owners (who took over from their father after he started the site back in the 1970s) are firmly against the corporate world of on-site shops, bustling bars and infinite rows of caravans. Instead they provide just a sprinkling of grassy shelves where you can pitch up, soak in the views and let the world gently amble by.

The Wee Camp Site hardly ever gets really busy, partly because there aren't enough pitches to apply the term appropriately and partly because few people actually make it here. The exception to this rule is one random week in summer, when a coach load of Czech campers who have been coming every year for as long as anyone can remember arrive at the site. If you manage to avoid them (perfectly nice as they may be), you may even have the place to yourself.

The unmarked pitches lie on the level terraces that ease down the hillside, allowing you to pitch where you want, though be careful to keep a respectable distance from your fellow campers; cosy Czechs aside, the Wee Camp Site is not keen on packing in tents sardine-style.

Through the trees that separate the site from the quiet village of Lochcarron, there are tempting views of the deep, blue expanse of Loch Carron itself. In the other direction, from the rear of the site, the views are of grassy foothills leading off into mountainous terrain. For hikers, the path at the back of the site opens up a massive expanse of unspoiled walks; you can stick to one of the narrow paths or sheep tracks, or simply blaze you own trail. It's a good idea to take all the necessary gear, as there will be nothing else up here but you, the sheep and, invariably, the wind.

Given the lack of facilities, or anything to do on the site, the village of Lochcarron tempts. Although not as popular as the tourist star of Plockton on the other side of the loch (itself well worth a visit if you have a car or a bike), Lochcarron is a pleasantly sleepy, wee place to while away the hours, with a

trim, whitewashed waterfront and a sprinkling of cosy cafés. It even has its own nine-hole golf course, which, though it will never stage the Open, has sweeping views of the mountains and lochs all around. In every direction are impossibly sturdy and rugged mountains, whether you're looking across at Attadale over the water or off to the west and the mountains of Applecross.

The proximity of the campsite to the western coast means that an essential activity around these parts is to tuck into impossibly plump and juicy langoustines, known simply as 'prawns' locally. They are so tasty and abundant that many are spirited off to the fine dining tables of London and Paris, though you can savour them locally at the Kishorn Seafood Bar.

The fact that the owners are not embracing mass-market tourism or exploiting peak-season campers with exorbitant rates is obvious as soon as you arrive and pay the bill (£8 a night for a family of four). So, it's a wee campsite with suitably wee prices.

THE UPSIDE: A wee, quiet campsite.

THE DOWNSIDE: Basic facilities; midges can be a problem in summer.

THE DAMAGE: £4 per person, children go free.

THE FACILITIES: Basic toilet and shower block with washing machine.

NEAREST DECENT PUB: The Lochcarron Hotel (01520 722226), on the main road in Lochcarron, has a decent range of pub grub and a popular beer garden. You won't go wrong if you stick to staples like fish and chips or the daily specials.

IF IT RAINS: Visit the nearby Kishorn Seafood Bar (01520 733240), 6 miles to the west in Kishorn, on the way to Applecross, for some of the freshest and best value seafood you'll taste anywhere in the UK. Well worth the drive or cycle. Alternatively, head to nearby Strathcarron and catch the scenic railway (08457 484950) to either Plockton or Inverness.

GETTING THERE: Heading north from Inverness on the A9 take the A835 towards Ullapool then the A832 towards Gairloch and the A890/A896 towards Lochcarron. As you enter the village look out for a sign on the right-hand side directing you to the campsite.

PUBLIC TRANSPORT: Catch the train from Inverness to Strathcarron (08457 484950). Highland Country Buses (01463 222244) operate the Strathcarron to Lochcarron service.

OPEN: Easter–Oct.

IF IT'S FULL: Unlikely, but if it is, try Applecross campsite (p171) nearby.

The Wee Camp Site, Dunrovin, Croft Road, Lochcarron, Wester Ross IV54 8YA t 01520 722898

applecross

Not many campsites are worth losing your car over. Applecross is one of them. This glorious escape lies well off the tourist trail, across the infamous Bealach na Ba, which is not so much a road as a rite of passage for Scots, a murderous mountain ordeal that soon sorts out the real cars from the old bangers. And that's exactly what happened on our first visit; our prehistoric Rover never recovered from the experience. But one of the first things we did with the new car was head straight back: Applecross is that sort of place.

The Bealach na Ba is Scotland's highest road, rising up from sea level to the top of the pass (625 metres high) in a series of hair-raising switchbacks. A large sign cautions that it is not a road for learner drivers and should not be attempted at all in wintry conditions, a message that Jeremy Clarkson types will no doubt just see as a challenge. To make things even more interesting, it is a single-track road with passing places at a premium. You'll not be alone if you find yourself saying your prayers as you 'negotiate' for space with oncoming cars (the locals tend to feel that

hurtling up and down with their eyes closed is the best plan) and the occasional kamikaze bus driver.

For the more cautious driver, there is a road in from the north of the Applecross Peninsula, but it takes a good hour and a half longer and does not have the same heart-stopping 'why-did-we-come-this-way-you-idiot!' drama attached. At the top of the Bealach na Ba, make sure to stop at the parking place, where an orientation board highlights the local landmarks and the multitude of islands and peaks that you can savour all around. That is, of course, if the weather is good; on a bad day you may need a compass just to get back to your car.

The campsite itself is handily located on the road that slaloms down towards the village from the mountain pass. Go past the first field by the reception as the views are better from the 'overflow' and there are no caravans there. Both fields are relatively flat with soft ground to pitch on and occupy a great position overlooking Applecross Bay. A deer fence does slightly detract from the view, but some enterprising souls sling

their camping chairs over the fence. From here you will get some of the finest views you will ever see of Scotland's largest island, the Isle of Skye, with its world famous and unmistakable Cuillin mountains. The site does have a few statics, a B&B and some wigwams to go along with the space for 60 tents, but it doesn't usually get too crowded, even at the height of summer, because of the effort required to get here.

Down in the tiny village (little more than a string of whitewashed houses clinging to the seafront) the highlight is the legendary Applecross Inn. This is the hub of the community where locals and visitors mingle over lobster and langoustines (called prawns up here) hauled ashore by the bloke sitting in the corner who now looks a bit worse for wear after a few too many celebratory pints of heavy ale. Yes, you can walk all around the Applecross Peninsula, go out on an adrenaline-filled RIB (rigid inflatable boat) ride and cruise around on a stately sea kayak, but most campers seem to prefer to split their time between the Inn and the campsite – while their cars sit sweating away in anticipation of the nightmare trip back across the Bealach na Ba.

THE UPSIDE: One of Scotland's most remote campsites enjoys a real end-of-the-world feel as well as views of the Isle of Skye.

THE DOWNSIDE: The walk back up the hill from the Applecross Inn.

THE DAMAGE: £6 per adult; under-16s free.

THE FACILITIES: Good toilets with hot showers and a laundry. The funky Flower Tunnel café serves food and drinks (both alcoholic and non-alcoholic); it also has a small play area and armchairs.

NEAREST DECENT PUB: Pubs just don't get any better than the Applecross Inn (01520 744262).

Enjoy fresh-from-the-boat seafood. Lobster, fresh beef and lamb are all regulars on the menu, with real ales on tap.

IF IT RAINS: Apart from the Applecross Inn, the Potting Shed Café is worth popping into, if only to see the Victorian walled garden they are trying to resurrect.

GETTING THERE: From Inverness, continue north on the A9, then the A835 towards Ullapool, followed by the A832 towards Gairloch and the A896 towards Lochcarron. Just past the village of Kishorn, turn left on to the Bealach na Ba, which is clearly signposted.

PUBLIC TRANSPORT: It's complicated to say the least. A postbus service runs from Shieldaig to Applecross once a day. Shieldaig in turn is connected to Strathcarron by postbus (08457 740740). Strathcarron can be reached from Inverness by train (08457 484950).

OPEN: All year (although don't even think about Bealach na Ba in snow or icy conditions).

IF IT'S FULL: Wild camping near the top of the Bealach na Ba (seriously). Also good wild camping by the beach in Applecross (p219).

Applecross Campsite, Applecross, Strathcarron, Wester Ross IV54 8ND

| | | t | 01520 744268 | w | www.applecross.uk.com/campsite |

sands holiday centre

First things first. Sands Holiday Centre has 150 tent pitches, 160 pitches for touring caravans and yes (come closer so no one else can hear), it is even home to 18 static caravans. But as you pitch amongst the machair, amidst voluminous sand dunes and linger at the epic view over the Atlantic to the Isle of Skye and the Outer Hebrides you will soon realise that despite its best efforts the Sands cannot help being a cool place to camp.

This spacious site is flanked by farmland on two sides and the Atlantic on another, with plenty of space even when it gets busy, as owners William and Moira Cameron insist that campers keep at least seven metres apart. There are no fixed pitches at Sands so you can set up your tent amongst the enormous dunes that separate the beach and the campsite. Caravans are banned from this part of the site, so campers really get the prime location and the most appealing views. As you turn your back on the caravans and take in the panorama of the Atlantic and the Outer Hebrides you will soon forget that your fellow campers even exist.

Facilities at the Sands Holiday Centre are plentiful if a little outdated. One of the toilet blocks has been modernised and has underfloor heating, which comes in handy during those cooler nights at the start of the season. A herd of Highland cattle and the Cameron's sheep are added attractions for children, but the real reason to camp here is Little Sands Beach.

Located adjacent to miles of sandy beach that is sheltered by the mass of Longa Island, it is no surprise that the Sands Holiday Centre is popular with watersports enthusiasts, who arrive with windsurf boards, sailing dinghies and kayaks in tow. The water temperature, somewhat cruelly, rarely rises above 12°C, so don't forget to pack a wetsuit or, even better, a dry suit if you want to spend more than just a few minutes splashing around in the sea. Strong Atlantic breezes can also whip up the waves and the beach does not have a lifeguard, so ensure that young children are supervised. For landlubbers, Little Sands is a quiet venue for a bracing stroll, for walking the dog or simply watching the world go by. Down on the beach, away from the delicate

ecosystem of the dunes, you are even welcome to light a campfire.

If you can bear to drag yourself away from Little Sands Beach make a beeline for the Inverewe Gardens, which are just nine miles away. When Osgood MacKenzie declared his intention to create a garden brimming with exotic plants from around the globe many of his contemporaries thought he'd taken leave of his senses (a belief that his daily skinny dip did nothing to dispel), particularly in light of the fact that his proposed site on the shore of Loch Ewe comprised mainly bedrock. His detractors, however, simply did not have the vision to

realise that the warm currents that passed through the loch from the Gulf Stream were ideal for what MacKenzie had in mind. Today the verdant gardens at Inverewe boast everything from Californian dog's-tooth violets to Chinese rhododendrons and are widely regarded as some of the most impressive in Britain.

Heading back to the Sands, the first thing you will see are caravans spread around the site, but this time you will know that up by the dunes lies a camping oasis and that soon you will be hunkering down on the beach enjoying a campfire with epic island and Highland views.

THE UPSIDE: Tent-only camping in the sand dunes.

THE DOWNSIDE: The 160 touring caravan pitches and 18 static caravans.

THE DAMAGE: Tent and car £9/£12 (low/high season); a two-person ridge tent is £8.50/£11 and bikers pay £3/£5. Additional tents cost £2/£5 and additional cars £2/£3.

THE FACILITIES: Hot showers, dishwashing area, electric hook-ups, laundry, payphones, games room, play area and licensed shop.

NEAREST DECENT PUB: Mustn't Grumble (01445 771212), 6 miles from the campsite at Melvaig, is a modern bar-restaurant with fresh local produce, lounge chairs and a big-screen television. The pan-seared scallops and the haddock are both highly recommended.

IF IT RAINS: The Gairloch Heritage Museum (01445 712287) openly welcomes casual visitors seeking shelter, as well as more serious scholars of history. The hands-on exhibits give a good insight into Highland life.

GETTING THERE: Take the A832 to Gairloch. From there follow the B8021 coastal road north towards Melvaig, the Sands Holiday Centre is 4 miles along this road on the left.

PUBLIC TRANSPORT: There is a daily bus from Inverness to Gairloch. From there you will need to walk or hitch a ride.

OPEN: Apr–Sep.

IF IT'S FULL: Try the Gairloch Caravan Park (01445 712373) 2 miles down the road in Strath.

Sands Holiday Centre, Gairloch, Wester Ross IV21 2DL	t	01445 712152	w	www.sandsholidaycentre.co.uk

northern lights

If someone is prepared to wait four years (and counting) to secure the planning permission to build their new home, then you know that they must have found a very special spot indeed. Mike and Ethel Elliot are content to spend each summer tending their intimate campsite from the confines of a small touring caravan and, despite the absence of the self-build property that they so desperately want to live in, welcome you to Northern Lights as if it were the home they don't yet have.

In less time than it took to pitch our tent, we understood why the Elliots were so dedicated to living in Badcaul. Set amidst classic Highland scenery where the mountains and coast enjoy a dramatic dalliance, Northern Lights offers breath-halting views over Little Loch Broom, Badrallach and the hulk of Beinn Ghobhlach. If that is not enough, the light changes as frequently as the weather, bringing out a rich palette of greens, blues, purples and greys.

Even the most sceptical visitors succumb to Badcaul's charm, as Ethel, who is an expert storyteller, explained to us. It was with just the right measure of humour and pride that she recounted the tale of a Cheshire man who complained bitterly on arrival that campsite was too small (it has just 12 pitches), that there was nothing to do in this cast-adrift outpost of Scotland and, worst of all, he couldn't get any reception on his television. The soap addict curtly informed Ethel he was going to leave, but was over-ruled by his wife who had instantly fallen in love with Badcaul. Four days later he too had been won over by the ever-changing moods of the mountains and loch, or perhaps it had been the passing Minke Whale he had run to tell Ethel about.

You've guessed it, despite missing a flurry of his essential soaps, our man from Cheshire ended up even more reluctant than his wife to leave after his epiphany. Whilst it is not guaranteed that you will stumble upon a whale, you have a high chance of spotting porpoises frolicking in the loch below, red deer strolling by the site and some of the whole host of birds who call this ruggedly beautiful natural environment home.

If you are not content to simply relax and enjoy the views then there are plenty of opportunities to get about the place. Walkers from around the globe are drawn to the Northern Lights campsite for the opportunity to tackle one of the better-known West Highland mountains, An Teallach. This imposing massif actually has three summits – Sail Lath (954 metres), Sgurr Fiona (1,060 metres) and Bidein a Ghlas Thuill (1,062 metres) – so there are plenty of choices and challenges. A less-strenuous alternative is to pick your way down to the rocky shores of Little Loch Broom.

Back at the site, Ethel and Mike have been working hard to upgrade the camping experience. They are currently renovating the toilet block, which is housed in a former croft, and now boasts new sink tops with a new tiled floor on the way. The rest of the simple campsite comprises a grassy field that slopes down towards the loch, with soft pitches opening up the views.

If, like the Elliots, you fall in love with this remote corner of Ross-shire, maybe you will find yourself dreaming of the day that the Highlands and Islands Council grant you permission to build a home overlooking Little Loch Broom. Until then you will just have to make do, like the Elliots, and enjoy it all from your temporary Highland home.

THE UPSIDE: The views – see instantly why the Elliots are so fond of this part of the world.

THE DOWNSIDE: There is no telephone or email on site, so if you want to book ahead you need to do it through the Larches Caravan Park in Cumbria, which is also owned by the Elliots.

THE DAMAGE: £5 for 1 person, £8 for 2 people and £2 per extra person.

THE FACILITIES: These are fairly rudimentary with toilets, metered hot showers (50p for 7 minutes), electrical hook-ups, a rotary clothesline and a dishwashing area.

NEAREST DECENT PUB: Located 15 miles away on the shore of Loch Ewe, the Aultbea Hotel & Restaurant (01445 731201) boasts good views and lovely seafood like dressed local crab and Loch Ewe scallops.

IF IT RAINS: Put on your waterproofs to brave the elements and enjoy a bracing low-level walk.

GETTING THERE: Heading north on the A9 from Inverness take the A835 to Ullapool then the A832 towards Gairloch, after around 10 miles you will reach the campsite.

PUBLIC TRANSPORT: The Westerbus (01445 712255) Gairloch–Inverness–Gairloch passes through Badcaul on Monday, Wednesday and Saturday.

OPEN: Apr–Sep.

IF IT'S FULL: Wild camp around the shores of Little Loch Broom, taking care not to annoy the local landowners, or head around the loch to Badrallach campsite (p189).

Northern Lights Campsite, Croft 9, Badcaul, Dundonnell, Ross-shire IV23 2QY

| t | 01697 371379 (Bookings via the Larches Caravan Park, Cumbria) | e | thelarches@hotmail.co.uk |

badrallach

You have to hand it to the Stott family. Not content with living in one of the most remote parts of the UK in the Shetland Isles, they decided in 1991 to up sticks completely and create what has to be one of Britain's most remote campsites. They wasted no time converting three old crofts into a top little campsite with a bothy (a basic communal shelter in a remote location) on hand, so others could share in some of the most epic scenery in Britain.

The Stott family (Mick, Ali, Titus, Cosmo and Percy the dog) have created a wee gem on the site of the former crofts. The setting they chose is sublime, tucked right on the shores of Little Loch Broom (actually fairly grand as it sweeps past the site towards its climactic meeting with the Atlantic) with a chunk of huge Highland peaks vying for attention all around. Getting here is interesting too, as you have to negotiate a vertiginous single-track road that would tax a rally driver, but it is well worth the effort.

The site, which takes only 12 tents, consists of a grassy field where many people choose to camp in summer to avoid the worst of the midges – although they installed a 'midgebuster' in 2004 the little devils can still be troublesome. If you visit outside of midge season, or if you are just feeling plain daft and are doused in a liberal soaking of Avon Skin So Soft (the only thing that ever seems to keep the little blighters at bay), then break away and choose one of the small private pitches set amidst the heather. Here you can create your own hidden Highland idyll complete with a campfire. The beach beckons just a short way down a pebbly track and is as popular with campers as it is with sun-worshipping seals.

When the rains sweep in there is the bothy – a rudimentary shelter set up in an old barn that you can sleep in with a sleeping bag or just come and use for shelter or eating. Bothies are an integral part of Scottish outdoor culture and this is your chance to sample 'bothy life' without having to trek miles to get there. If you choose to stay here you can hire it exclusively; it's perfect for walkers as there is a peat stove you can cosy down around after a hard day in the hills.

The surrounding area is massively and deservedly popular with the walking community as there are countless peaks within easy reach, although you will need a car to get to the base of most. A Stott family

favourite is An Teallach, a massive Munro that pokes over a kilometre high above the loch. Non-walkers can also hire out kayaks to paddle around the loch, rent bikes to explore the peninsula or try to take control of one of the power kites that take full advantage of the Atlantic winds. There is also bountiful salmon, sea trout and brown trout fishing on the brace of local estates.

It must have been hard to leave Shetland, but if you're going to move anywhere, then Badrallach is a pretty good choice. And in a moment of clarity – perhaps during a night spent around the camp fire, with only the gentle lapping of Little Loch Broom and a shadow of Highland peaks for company – you will possibly find yourself agreeing with the Stott's romanticism that this is truly 'a timeless place'.

THE UPSIDE: You can see why the Stotts left Shetland behind.

THE DOWNSIDE: Midges can be lethal in the heather; few wet-weather options for those without a car.

THE DAMAGE: A wonderfully cheap £3 per person and £2.50 for a tent.

THE FACILITIES: Good facilities (electricity arrived in 2002) with hot showers, a public telephone and decent toilets. Shelter in the bothy.

NEAREST DECENT PUB: The Dundonnell Hotel (01854 633204) is as close as you get, but still a slow drive down the Badrallach road and then a mile or two further around the loch. The Broombeg Bar here awaits with pub grub, whilst classier fare is on offer in the Claymore Restaurant with lamb, beef and venison dishes.

IF IT RAINS: Head to the bothy and cosy up by the peat fire.

GETTING THERE: Take the A9 north from Inverness onto the A835 to Ullapool. Approximately 10 miles from Ullapool at Braemore Junction turn left onto the A832 for 10 miles then turn right onto the single track Badrallach road for 7 miles.

PUBLIC TRANSPORT: The Westerbus (01445 712255) Gairloch–Inverness–Gairloch passes the road end (7 miles) on Monday, Wednesday and Saturday.

OPEN: All year.

IF IT'S FULL: Wild camp around the shores of Little Loch Broom, taking care not to annoy the local landowners, or skip around the loch to another *Cool Camping* favourite the Northern Lights campsite (p183).

Badrallach, Croft 9, Badrallach, Dundonnell, Ross-Shire IV23 2QP

| t | 01854 633281 | w | www.badrallach.com |

ardmair point

All right, first things first. Ardmair Point is next to a road, it has over a hundred pitches and a quintet of wooden chalets and caravans enjoy the best waterfront positions. But – and this is a big but – the site enjoys one of the most spectacular locations of any in Europe. Set adrift on its own peninsula, the Atlantic laps at three sides, the Coigach ridge rises impossibly steeply just to the north and the famed Summer Isles tempt on the horizon. Oh, and the fishing port of Ullapool, with its great pubs and great food is just three miles down the road.

The first thing you will probably notice at Ardmair are the views with sea, hills and islands all around. The efficient reception block as you enter has a well-stocked shop, with everything from local maps and waterproofs through to kites and butteries – a strange east coast 'delicacy'. If you are not lucky enough to have been force-fed them as a child and brainwashed into thinking you still have to eat them as an adult, imagine 100 croissants with a layer of lard laced between each, then squashed in an industrial vice and you will have something

approaching the artery-clogging reality of butteries. Eat one and you won't need to eat again for weeks.

The campsite offers a choice of areas to pitch on. There is the main grassy field, which has a gentle slope, but does not have any caravans. Most tenters head there, though watch where you pitch as there is some stony ground. Arguably the best position is in the small clearing just below the site's highest point, though the midges tend to be in residence here when there is no breeze.

One of the most unusual aspects of Ardmair is that you can bring your own boat along on a trailer – or even arrive by boat if you like. Moorings are free, so you can sail up here and use it is a base or just launch your boat off the slip and potter around the wide bay. Kayaks are also welcome with some top-notch paddling around this rugged indented coastline, with its challenging Atlantic swells and unpredictable currents. Land-based attractions include Ullapool Golf Club just down the road; not exactly championship quality but a fun course nonetheless. This being the Highlands there are numerous opportunities for walks, whether you are looking for a gentle stroll or a challenging adventure. Then, of course, there are the cruises out to the Summer Isles from Ullapool.

Ullapool itself is a major pull, a working port where real fishermen still drink real beer in real pubs. In this unpretentious little town, you can order a coffee in the tearoom and take it outside on their 'terrace' – which happens to be the harbour wall, with impressive views of Loch Broom and the brooding hills. The harbour wall also forms the beer garden of the best pub in town, the Ferry Boat Inn.

Back at Ardmair, there can be a bit of traffic noise during the day and you'll certainly be aware of the caravans and chalets around, but by night as you savour a moonlit stroll along the pebble beach any reservations about Ardmair soon disappear. Many visitors will die happy having experienced that viewscape. But beware: eat too many butteries and that might be a lot sooner than you expect.

THE UPSIDE: Stunning location with sea and hill views just a stone's throw from one of Scotland's most enjoyable fishing ports.

THE DOWNSIDE: Caravans, tourers and the wooden chalets get the best views.

THE DAMAGE: £11–17 for a tent, car and two people; £7 for a lone camper travelling on foot.

THE FACILITIES: Modern facilities block (Scandinavian-style chalet) with washing machine, dryers, hot showers and hairdryers, electric hook-ups.

NEAREST DECENT PUB: Ferry Boat Inn (01854 612366). Real ales, 'haggis, neeps and tatties' and local Lochinver haddock are on the menu in a pub where the craic flows as freely as the beer. Perhaps a bit too lively for some tastes at weekends.

IF IT RAINS: Grab a slice of Highland culture and a slice of cake at Ceilidh Place (01854 612103; www.ceilidhplace.com). This café, restaurant, hotel, bookshop and ceilidh venue (informal gathering with live folk music and dancing) has been at the heart of Ullapool life since 1970.

GETTING THERE: From Inverness take the A835 towards Ullapool. The campsite is located on the left, 3 miles north of Ullapool.

PUBLIC TRANSPORT: Spa Coaches (01997 421311) run the N71 from Ullapool to Ardmair.

OPEN: May–Sep.

IF IT'S FULL: Wild camping by the lochs en route to Achiltibuie (p219), or try the Cool Camping site at Achnahaird Farm (p199).

| Ardmair Point, Ardmair, Ullapool, Ross-shire IV26 2TN | t | 01854 612054 | w | www.ardmair.com |

achnahaird farm

Some marketing-savvy campsites like to wax lyrical about their remote locations and boast of being lost 'on the road to nowhere'. Achnahaird Farm doesn't. In fact, this unpretentious farm campsite does not really market itself at all. And anyway, more accurately, it is 10 miles along the road to nowhere on one of Scotland's most spectacular wee roads, which breaks off the main Ullapool to John O'Groats 'highway' and plunges deep into the mountains on a sinewy loch-strewn trail.

Theoretically, you can travel at 60mph along the single-track road to nowhere, but the stubborn, daredevil sheep, the hairy, brake-testing bends and the camera-teasing views combine to ensure you will probably slug along at a more soporific 10mph. Some would-be campers don't even manage to complete the journey as the trio of lochs you pass en route are perfect for wild camping, with a string of bijou sandy beaches set amidst the heather.

You won't find a glossy colour brochure at Achnahaird telling you all about the wide range of facilities and the flurry of local visitor attractions – there are few facilities and few attractions as such, bar the swathe of epic Highland mountain scenery and the wide sweep of Achnahaird beach. This is the sort of place where you spend half your time quietly congratulating yourself on discovering it, as you recline with your favourite tipple, checking and re-checking the sublime views just to make sure they are still there. You may want to do the same with your tent on a windy day; although, mercifully the firm but sandy soil allows you to dig those pegs in deep.

Finding somewhere to set up your tent on the wide 30-pitch site is easy, with no designated sites; the most popular spots are closest to the beach. Wherever you choose, a nice touch is owner Marilyn MacKenzie's personal visit to new arrivals. She may take your money but you will get a genuinely warm welcome in return.

Active types will want to tackle the hulking local mountains with two of Scotland's most celebrated peaks, Stac Pollaidh and Suliven, stretching up across the sands in the distance. Both are unmistakable: Stac

Pollaidh with its rugged pinnacles bursting skywards and the stately chunk of Suliven overseeing the scene. Stac Pollaidh is not for those without a head for heights or some experience of rock scrambling, but there are plenty of smaller hills for campers looking for a gentler ramble.

Four miles on from Achnahaird and a flurry of obstructive sheep and a silvery loch later you finally find the end of the road to nowhere in nowhere itself, Achiltibuie. This isolated wee hamlet is impressively home to one of the Highlands' best hotels, the Summer Isles, and one of the country's only soil-less hydroponicums. Here you can enjoy the surreal experience of enjoying fresh

'Highland Bananas'. You can even take a hydroponicum starter park away to scare your friends with when you get back home; they also come highly recommended as an obscure present to confuse elderly relatives.

The sunsets in Achiltibuie are justly famous, but those at Achnahaird Farm are equally impressive, with most campers drawn down to the water. The number one spot is on the rocks by the beach where you can savour the sun melting over the Outer Hebrides in a burst of fiery reds and deep oranges. Don't forget your torch, though, as trekking back up the road to nowhere is even harder without a light.

THE UPSIDE: Gorgeous beach and mountain views that will have you wandering around aimlessly with your mouth wide open.

THE DOWNSIDE: Basic facilities with no showers, camping shelter or shop; no lights in the toilet block either so don't forget your torch.

THE DAMAGE: £7 per 2-person tent then £1 extra per adult and 50p per child.

THE FACILITIES: Decent toilet block with only cold water. Hot showers available for £1 in Achiltibuie Village Hall.

NEAREST DECENT PUB: The Summer Isles Bar (01854 622282; www.summerisleshotel.co.uk), in Achiltibuie, is lauded for its excellent seafood; the even more celebrated restaurant next door offers one of the finest culinary experiences in Scotland at £51 for a 5-course set menu.

IF IT RAINS: Cruises from nearby run to the Summer Isles, fittingly summer only, whilst locals insist rainy days are not for mountains but are perfect for coastal walks along the old sheep tracks that snake away from the beach.

GETTING THERE: From Inverness take the A835 towards Ullapool. Ten miles north of Ullapool turn left onto the single-track road signed to Achiltibuie. Ten miles further on a camping symbol points the way to the campsite. The entrance is just past the farm on the right.

OPEN: Apr–Sep.

IF IT'S FULL: Wild camping by the nearby lochs (p219) is an alternative, whilst the plush rooms of the Summer Isles Hotel (see left) provide accommodation at the other end of the scale.

Achnahaird Farm, Achnahaird, Achiltibuie, Ross-shire IV26 2YT   t 01854 622348   e achnahairdfarm@scotnet.co.uk

scourie

Robert Burns, Scotland's great mythologiser of the mundane and the simple, wrote odes to such humdrum things as mice, lice and haggis. But he never eulogised the Scottish midge and with good reason. Midges are neither soft and furry nor very appetising. Besides, 'wee sleekit cow'rin' tim'rous *chironomidae*' doesn't scan very well.

Whereas many of Scotland's coastal campsites are too windy for midges, the sheltered bay at Scourie does unfortunately provide ideal flying conditions for the little pests. However, that is no reason not to come and enjoy one of the most tranquil sites in Sutherland. This is one of the most sparsely populated regions of Europe and the scattered dwellings of the region's few human habitations seem to cling to the coast for safety.

Scourie is a tiny hamlet clustered around an inlet on the extreme northwest coast, 40 miles from Ullapool. The landscape here may be stark and sparse but the campsite is a little oasis of green. At first glance, you'd be forgiven for mistaking the green terraces for a nine-hole pitch-and-putt course, so immaculate is the grass. Caravans and motorhomes are largely confined to the areas around the amenities block, so tents have the run of the terraced pitches that extend down almost to the shores of the bay.

Scourie is an ideal stopping off point between Ullapool and the far north coast around Durness, 25 miles from Scourie. From Durness, a coastal village that seems like something blown north from Cornwall by Doomsday winds, a tiny boat takes you across the Kyle of Durness to rendezvous with a minibus that plies the only stretch of road in Britain not connected to any other road. It runs the 11 miles through an area called the Parph out to Cape Wrath, the most northeasterly point of the mainland and the site of a Stevenson lighthouse (see p209). It's a favourite haunt of kite surfers who can be seen from the cliff tops clinging to their kites as the winds try to whisk them to Spitzbergen.

For the intrepid there is a chillingly remote coastal walk from the crumbly chocolate cliffs of Cape Wrath back to the road from Kinlochbervie. The walk takes in the fantastic beach at Sandwood Bay and is so remote that it would make even Greta Garbo crave some company. The landscape here is not so much mountainous as pock-marked with massive towers of stone rising out of moorland. Maybe that is why the Ministry of Defence uses much of the area as a bombing target. These distinct mountains must be easy for even the greenest trainee pilot to hit.

Heading south from Scourie towards Ullapool is the impressive Loch Assynt with the forlorn ruin of Ardvreck Castle sitting exposed to the whipping winds that sweep up the length of the loch. In 1650, the Marquis of Montrose, who had continued to fight for Charles I, even after his execution in 1649, was led from here, trussed and bound to a horse, to Edinburgh for execution. He was placed on his horse backwards and

would have had a magnificent view of the receding castle as he was led away. Forty years later, the castle was ruined after a siege and left as it stands today, an empty but imposing shell.

After the sparseness of Sutherland, Ullapool feels like a metropolis. It's a small but bustling town and the main ferry route to the Outer Hebrides. Fresh fish is landed by a small fleet of brightly coloured trawlers, so it's no surprise that Ullapool also boasts the best chippy in Britain, as voted by the discerning listeners of Radio 4. It's known, appropriately enough, as The Chippy, a name whose simplicity Robert Burns would no doubt have admired.

THE UPSIDE: Peace and tranquillity amidst the west coast's rugged beauty.

THE DOWNSIDE: The pitches can retain rainwater like Balinese rice terraces.

THE DAMAGE: Tent, car and one adult starts at £8.50; tent and cyclist is £6; two motorbikes, one tent and two adults is £10. Phone for further permutations.

FACILITIES: One tired but clean toilet block with hot showers. Dishwashing and laundry also available. There is a small supermarket and an expensive petrol station in Scourie.

NEAREST DECENT PUB: The Scourie Hotel (01971 502396), 2 minutes' walk away, serves real ale (with a changing selection of guest ales) and decent pub grub but in a rather fatigued setting.

IF IT RAINS: Birds fly in the rain so take the boat to Handa Island (01971 502347) to watch the puffins, fulmers and shags.

GETTING THERE: From Ullapool follow the A834 north to Ledmore Junction and turn left onto the A837. Along the shores of Loch Assynt, turn right up the hill onto the A894 and it's another 17 miles to Scourie. A bus service runs north from Inverness via Ullapool and up the A838 to Scourie.

OPEN: Mar–Sep.

IF IT'S FULL: Head north to Durness where a dramatic campsite (01971 511262) overlooks Sango Sands or south to Ardmair (p195), just north of Ullapool to camp by the shores of Loch Broom.

| **Scourie Caravan & Camping**, Harbour Road, Scourie, Sutherland IV27 4TG | t | 01971 502060 |

dunnet bay

When you take it at face value, this site should be everything that cool camping is not: a Council-owned site; run by the Caravan Club, with wardens Adam and Jennifer Duff in mint-green Caravan Club uniforms; rules are everywhere. Yet, this small site is something of a gem. For a start, it was the first Caravan Club site to allow tents, marking a small victory for coloured canvas over beige fibreglass. The Club has also paid for an immaculate upgrade of all the facilities. But, more importantly, the site is jammed against the sand dunes of a sweeping bay. Long stalks of dune grass practically reach over a small wooden fence to touch your tent.

The restless waves of the Pentland Firth attract surfers from far and wide. But Dunnet Bay is one of the north coast's trump cards. With a mile or more of white sand stretching like a crescent moon to the cliffs of Dunnet Head, the most northerly point of mainland Britain, it's a spectacular setting. With a bit of sunshine, a few tinnies of beer and the odd shout of 'Ripper, mate!' you could swear you were on Bondi Beach in Australia. Well, almost.

For those with a head for heights, there's a road roaming for five miles over bleak and brown scrubland up towards the cliff top at Dunnet Head. Up there are the lighthouse built by Robert Louis Stevenson's grandfather and the ghostly remains of a World War II radar station, long since abandoned to the elements. The lighthouse looks out over Gill's Bay to the Orkneys, overseeing the channel between the headland and Scapa Flow, and is perilously close to crumbling into the sea. On a clear day, you can see the breadth of Scotland from up here – from Cape Wrath in the east to John O'Groats in the west. On a windy day (and let's face it, that's most days 100 metres up a cliff at the northernmost point of the mainland), you can listen to the moan of the wind whistling through the old radar station and try to imagine what it must have been like to be stationed here in the 1940s, with only the lighthouse keeper and a few puffins for company. Now the lighthouse keeper has gone – the light was automated some years ago – the radar watchers are no more and even the puffins have become elusive.

Virtually everywhere in northern Scotland is haunted by ghosts from the past and you can catch a sense of them in Dunnet Forest, a few minutes walk from the campsite. A range of trails snakes through a surprising variety of thick pine, open meadow and forest clearings. Those with an eye for such things might spot a Scottish primrose or some creeping willow and the odd dark green fritillary butterfly. Further into the forest are the remains of a Bronze Age hut circle from 3,500 years ago and a few totem poles decorated by local schoolchildren. In classic Blue Peter fashion, the masks on the poles are made from the tops of old washing-up bottles and billy cans.

Pinned to a tree nearby is a poem written by a primary school class about singing songs to the ghosts of the people who have gone. As the sun sets, it can feel a little eerie, like a scene from the *Blair Witch Project*. But luckily, the trails are well marked and the call of the waves is enough to prevent you being lured deeper and deeper into the thick dark woods.

Back out in the blustery evening sunlight, there's still time to grab your board and head out for one last blast through the surf before you settle down to dreams of bagging one of those elusive puffins.

THE UPSIDE: Beautiful sandy bay and grassy dunes.

THE DOWNSIDE: Site is mainly for caravans and has relatively few pitches for tents.

THE DAMAGE: Varies with the season. High season is £5 per person plus £2 for a small tent or £4 for a large.

THE FACILITIES: Immaculately refurbished toilets and hot showers. Dishwashing & laundry facilities also available.

NEAREST DECENT PUB: The lounge bar at the Northern Sands Hotel (01847 851270), half a mile away, has leather chairs and wood panelling and serves a decent pint and excellent sandwiches. For those who want a little more rock with their roll, head into Thurso to Top Joe's at the Central Hotel.

IF IT RAINS: Visit Mary-Anne's cottage in Dunnet village. It's an old croft, left intact after the death of its 93-year-old owner – and she had kept it just as her grandfather had it.

GETTING THERE: Follow the A836 for 7 miles from Thurso to the sands of Dunnet Bay. The site is between the road and the dunes.

PUBLIC TRANSPORT: A regular daily bus service runs from Thurso to Dunnet (except Sundays).

OPEN: Mar–Sep.

IF IT'S FULL: There is a campsite in Thurso if required but for a little extra cash, there are nine rooms at the cosy and comfortable Northern Sands Hotel (see above), ranging from £35 per night single to up to £70 per night double.

Dunnet Bay Caravan and Camping Site, Dunnet, Thurso KW14 8XD   t   01847 821319

betty mouat's böd

On stressful 21st century days with mobiles beeping, wireless networks blinking and iPods thumping, things can all get a bit much. What price, then, the chance to leave the modern world behind and escape to a chain of islands blessed with 100 beaches where you can camp in a 19th-century stone böd (stone cottage) surrounded by the ghosts of the wonderfully mysterious Betty Mouat, a woman whose epic story of survival makes office stresses and strains seem trivial in comparison?

Shetland is littered with a legacy of old böds. These are traditional croft buildings used to house fishermen and their gear, and keep them safe from the wild Atlantic weather systems that tend to sweep in at a moment's notice in this tumultuous part of the world. Since 1992 many of these have been converted to provide basic accommodation for campers not keen to risk wild camping and full exposure to the elements. Betty Mouat's Böd is very basic and has no electricity – you will need to bring your own sleeping bag as well as eating and cooking utensils. This is no youth hostel with a helpful warden on hand and a welcoming bar, but located over a wild stretch of barren landscape and the turbulent waters of the Atlantic, the böd has to be one of the most atmospheric places to stay in Britain.

Betty Mouat was born in Levenwick in 1825, the only child of fisherman Thomas Mouat. She went on to have three children, living to a ripe old age of 93, but the most dramatic episode in Betty's life came in 1886 when, in her sixties, she was left abandoned on a ship, the *Columbine*. During a fierce storm, the crew were set adrift after a failed attempt to rescue the vessel's captain and Betty was left alone on the ship. Few gave her any hope of survival but she and the *Columbine* pitched up a week later across the sea in Norway. She spent her remaining years enthralling a steady stream of visitors with her impressive tales of survival on nothing else but milk and her iron will.

It is fitting that today Betty's old home now offers refuge to new arrivals who wash up on these distant shores. Just a short drive or walk, from Shetland's international airport (flights to Norway, the Faroe Islands as well as Scotland and England), the böd makes a perfect base for exploring the islands.

Recently an old broch tower was unearthed right next door and the chances are that when you stay there will be an archaeological team working away on the site, stripping back the layers of an island that has been settled since prehistoric times. There is a real sense of being part of history here and if you are keen, they may let you help out on the dig.

Just down the road is an even more impressive ancient site that has been comprehensively excavated. At Jarlshof, humankind's imprint has been traced back 4,000 years with Bronze Age and Iron Age remnants still visible today, though the most telling legacy is that of the Vikings, who once rampaged through Scotland's northerly isles. You can tour their 9th-century longhouses and conjure up images of their long ships floating just offshore. In the Shetland Isles, history is not treated as something to be shut away in a hermetically sealed museum exhibit – you can ramble all over the site piecing it all together for yourself, an experience as far away from the stresses and strains of modern city life as you can imagine.

THE UPSIDE: The chance to cosy up in an old crofting house surrounded by the ghosts of Betty Mouat.

THE DOWNSIDE: Right on the southern tip of the Shetland mainland so you really need your own car for getting further afield.

THE DAMAGE: £8 per person per night (maximum 10 people).

THE FACILITIES: Hot-water heater, shower, 2 bedrooms and 3 public rooms.

NEAREST DECENT PUB: It is a bit of a journey, but the trip to Shetland's capital of Lerwick is worth it for the Queens Hotel (01595 692826;

www.kgqhotels.co.uk). Choose from the snug bar or the informal restaurant with its top-notch seafood and sea views.

IF IT RAINS: It's back to the Queens Hotel (see above) for a room when the weather closes in. Lerwick also has good pubs, shop and the funky new Shetland Museum (www.shetland-museum.org.uk).

GETTING THERE: British Airways (www.britishairways.co.uk) fly direct to Shetland from Glasgow, Edinburgh and Aberdeen. Atlantic Airways (www.atlantic.fo) fly direct from London Stansted.

PUBLIC TRANSPORT: Public transport is not exactly set up with tourists in mind, more to keep the numerous islands in the archipelago connected for locals. There are fairly regular buses from the airport to Lerwick, which pass right by the böd, run by Leask & Son (01595 693162).

OPEN: Apr–Sep.

IF IT'S FULL: There are seven other böds dotted around the Shetland Isles (www.camping-bods.com), or you can wild camp in the dunes behind the numerous sandy beaches (p219).

| **C/o VisitShetland**, Market Cross, Lerwick, Shetland ZE1 0LU | t | 01595 693434 | w | www.camping-bods.com |

wild camping

Ask some Scottish campers which campsite they prefer and you might get a funny look. For real outdoor types, 'wild camping' is the only way to go – just choosing a suitably remote spot in the countryside to pitch your tent. Wild camping offers an incredible sense of freedom that no organised site can ever hope to match, though, of course, the downside is that there are no facilities; fine as you cosy down at sunset with a wee dram, but not so appealing on a groggy wet morning. Scotland has long enjoyed a relatively liberal attitude to campers and land access compared with England and Wales, but such freedoms were enshrined in law by the Land Reform (Scotland) Act 2003.

While the law affords you the freedom to camp sensibly anywhere (within reason), it doesn't mean you can just pitch up in someone's garden and refuse to budge. Freedom brings with it responsibilities, none of which are very burdensome, but all of which are designed for maximum camping enjoyment and minimum impact. Useful general 'rules' are: not to camp anywhere for more than three nights; avoid enclosed fields, active hunting estates and residential areas; stay low down in a glen rather than on exposed and fragile upper ground; and avoid fires, as spreading them is a risk at any time of year. You should also be careful to stay away from nesting birds and avoid attracting birds of prey with food scraps, so dispose of all your waste diligently. Never choose a toilet spot within 30 metres of a water course and bury excrement in a small hole rather than just under a boulder. Finally, and most obviously, don't forget to remove all your litter.

Don't think that 'No Camping' signs are just crude attempts to circumnavigate the vagaries of the Land Reform Act as they may well be there for a good reason. Making the right choices with wild camping is largely a matter of common sense, but it's also worth seeking local advice; a quick chat to a farmer might well uncover a far better camping spot than you might have found. If you follow the old adage of 'taking only photos and leaving only footprints' (or in this case, shallow tent marks in areas that can recover easily), you shouldn't go far wrong.

The Mountaineering Council of Scotland has some helpful rough guidelines on-line (www.mountaineering-scotland.org.uk/leaflets/wildcamp.html) and they also publish a free leaflet on wild camping, which is very useful when planning a trip.

Wild camping is not for everyone, but once you've experienced the glorious freedom of finding that spectacular spot – and having it all to yourself – you may find yourself addicted. Here are a few recommended locations to get you started, but be a tiny bit brave and no doubt you'll find your own special places...

CALGARY BAY, ISLE OF MULL

In the main, Mull is a beautiful, unspoilt place with an almost bewildering variety of bewitching scenery. The wildest and most remote parts of the island lie the furthest from the ferry terminal on the west and north coasts of Mull. One of the most beautiful scenes, in the furthest flung corner, is the astonishing white sand beach at Calgary Bay. Responsible wild camping is actually encouraged here, right on the water's edge, and the hospitality extends to an adjacent water supply, waste bin and toilet. Although this is 'not so wild camping', in reality, just to be here, in these startling surroundings, is a rare privilege.

Nearest station: Oban, next to the ferry terminal.

GLEN ETIVE

Wild camping heaven; just leave the main road up towards the isles and tumble down the glen towards Glencoe and you enter a world where man feels very small indeed. Choose your spot and enjoy an amphi-theatre of towering Highland peaks, lush heather, deer strewn glens and gushing burns (streams). Glencoe itself boasts the famous Clachaig Inn (p82), and the busy hub of Fort William is less than an hour's drive away.

Nearest Station: Rannoch Railway Station.

Calgary Bay
Wild Camping Code

CLEAR AREA

TENTS ONLY

VEHICLES ONLY

 toilets

 YOU ARE HERE

House

House

Calgary Bay is owned by Argyll and Bute Council.

This is not an official campsite but wild camping is permitted.
Wild camping means short stay camping only.
Our aim is to protect and conserve this beautiful area for the enjoyment of all.

FIRES Please do not gather wood from nearby woodland. Use existing hearths - no fires on the machair. Driftwood and bought wood available locally.

WATER Please note that tap water or burn water is not fit for drinking.

RUBBISH Please clear up after your stay. Where possible, take rubbish away.

NOISE Please respect and consider others. Keep noise down, especially after 10.00pm

DOGS Please remember to keep your dog under control.

FLORA This is a protected area, please take care not to damage the vegetation.

Donations for the upkeep of the Bay received at the Carthouse, Calgary Hotel.
Thank you for keeping Calgary Bay special.

APPLECROSS

There is a flat grassy terrace right on the edge of the beach at this idyllic little village. Take the highest road in Scotland (the Bealach na Ba) and enjoy camping with a view of the Atlantic and the isles of Skye and Raasay in the distance. You can also camp at the top of the Bealach na Ba if you're brave. The legendary Applecross Inn (p174), with its top-notch seafood (langoustines and lobster are regulars) is a 15-minute walk from the beach.

Nearest Station: Strathcarron Train Station.

ACHILTIBUIE AND THE COIGACH PENINSULA

This wild Highland getaway enjoys both Atlantic views and some of Europe's most unique mountainscapes in the form of Suliven and Stac Pollaidh. Camp near the main road on one of the sandy beaches that fringe the freshwater lochs and enjoy the wilderness safe in the knowledge that the welcoming arms of Summer Isles Bar (p200) in Achiltibuie are within easy reach.

Nearest Station: Garve Railway Station.

HARRIS

Harris is one of the most wildly beautiful 'islands' (it is technically joined on to Lewis by a narrow isthmus) in Scotland. You can camp on the wild west coast alongside impossibly attractive sandy beaches with only seals and wild birds for company. The east coast is a curious netherworld of volcanic scenery that looks like nowhere else in the British Isles. This is real end-of-the-world stuff, so come prepared.

Nearest Airport: Stornoway Airport.

SHETLAND

The most northerly isles in the UK are blessed with around 100 gorgeous Atlantic beaches, not to mention swathes of history and bountiful flora and fauna. Check that it is fine locally and then just pitch up a tent by your own slice of beach heaven; although you will have to batten down the hatches in bad weather. The easiest places to get to are on the 'mainland', but there are even more remote spots on some of the surrounding isles and islets only a ferry or flight away.

Nearest Airport: Sumburgh Airport.

top tips

First timer? Take a minute to read our top tips. Most of it's just common sense, but you never know what you don't know.

BE PREPARED

More than just a motto! Make sure you've thought through everything you need to take. If it's your first time, make a thorough checklist before you go. You can download a handy checklist at www.coolcamping.co.uk

CHOOSE A GOOD SITE

Well obviously, it should be a campsite recommended by *Cool Camping*. But within the site, choose exactly where you pitch your tent carefully. Opt for level ground, ideally with some shade, too – tents get very hot in direct sunshine. But make sure your level ground isn't at the bottom of a big dip that will fill with water if it rains. Also, try to pick a place that's near enough to the amenities to be handy, but far enough to be free from associated noise and traffic.

AVOID SCHOOL HOLIDAYS

Don't go during busy periods if you can help it. Your experience and enjoyment will be greatly enhanced. If you can only go during school holidays, try to opt for quieter sites off the beaten track.

LEAVE NO TRACE

Dispose of your rubbish in the right place, only light fires in designated areas, respect the countryside and don't hassle or feed the wildlife. Lecture over!

A FEW WORDS OF WARNING

WALKING

Walking in Scotland can be dangerous – apparently, more people come a cropper every year on Ben Nevis than on Everest, so be aware of the potential hazards before setting out. Check and double check the weather conditions, take adequate gear, seek local advice and use common sense. For more information on walking in Scotland, see www.walking.visitscotland.com.

WILD CAMPING

Although wild camping is increasingly common in Scotland, please respect the environment and, wherever possible, check with local residents before pitching. *Cool Camping* cannot accept any responsibility for injuries caused by angry landowners or by any other means while wild camping.

happy campers?

The campsites featured in this book are a personal selection chosen by the Cool Camping team. None of the campsites has paid a fee for inclusion, nor was one requested, so you can be sure of an objective choice of sites and honest descriptions.

We have visited hundreds of campsites across Scotland to find the ones selected here, and we hope you like them as much as we do. However, it hasn't been possible to visit every single campsite. So, if you know of a special campsite that you think should be included, we'd like to hear about it.

Send us an email telling us the name and location of the campsite, some contact details and why it's special. We'll credit all useful contributions in the next edition of Cool Camping and the best emails will receive a complimentary copy. Feel free to tell us about campsites in England, Wales and anywhere else. Just use the relevant email details below. Thanks, and enjoy our great countryside. See you out there!

scotland@coolcamping.co.uk
england@coolcamping.co.uk
wales@coolcamping.co.uk
france@coolcamping.co.uk

Design and artwork: Andrew Davis
www.andrewjamesdavis.com
andrew@andrewjamesdavis.com

Series Concept & Series Editor:
Jonathan Knight

Researched and written by: Robin
McKelvie, Jenny McKelvie, Andy Stothert
and Keith Didcock
Editorial: Nikki Sims, Shellani Gupta &
Rachel Simmonds
Production: Catherine Greenwood,
Andrew Davis
Online: Andy Clarke
PR: Carol Farley, Farley Partnership
Coordinator-in-Chief: Catherine Greenwood

Published by:
Punk Publishing Ltd,
3 The Yard, Pegasus Place, London, SE11 5SD

Distributed by:
Portfolio Books, Suite 3/4,
Great West House, Great West Road,
Brentford, Middlesex TW8 9DF

All photographs © Robin McKelvie/Jenny
McKelvie/Andy Stothert/Keith Didcock
except the following, all reproduced with
kind permission; Marthrown of Mabie (p6,
p26, p29) © Marthrown of Mabie;
Strathfillan Wigwams (p56) © Strathfillan
Wigwams; White water rafters at
Grandtully (p70, p71, p73) © Fergus Duncan
(fergus@ziplockk.com); Happy campers
(p220) © Jason Bryant.

Front cover; Wild camping at Calgary Bay,
Mull © Andy Stothert

Many of the photographs featured in this
book are available for licensing. For more
information, see www.coolcamping.co.uk

Punk Publishing takes its environmental
responsibilities seriously. This book has
been printed on paper made from
renewable sources and we continue to work
with our printers to reduce our overall
environmental impact. Wherever possible,
we recycle, eat organic food and always
turn the tap off when brushing our teeth.

A BIG THANK YOU!
Thanks to everyone who has written in and
emailed with feedback, comments and
suggestions. It's good to see so many
people at one with the *Cool Camping* ethos.
In particular, thanks to the following
readers for telling us about their favourite
places to camp: **Phil Lewis, Mark
Hopgoodwalsh, Helen Smith, Rachel
Polhill, Rabhya Dewshi, Iain Harper, Gary
Lawes, Francis Saunders, Chris Gill, Lee
Roberts, Kathie Jessup and Emma Ives.**